MW00625837

My brother Jeff was recently asked how long a particular sermon took to prepare. "About 40 years," was his reply. There's something to that. This book of meditations for prayer wasn't prepared over weeks or months. There's a lifetime of lessons here. That's not to say that the three writers are great examples of faithful prayer. We'd all object to that, vehemently! But prayer is something we have learned—we *are learning*—through a lifetime of Bible study, and sin, and confession, and anxiety, and dependence. And mercifully and mightily, God answers, in spite of us.

I'm grateful for a father who modeled prayer, especially prayers of adoration. I thank God for giving me a love for private prayer as a teenager, especially for the sweet times kneeling each week in an empty church building (which I was supposed to be cleaning). I'm grateful that I learned early in my ministry as a church planting pastor that I am utterly dependent on God to do what I cannot. I grieve at my prayerlessness, but I can say with humility and certainty that my need for God's grace is an ever-present reality in my life. And so I pray.

I'm grateful for Carl Trueman, one of the most insightful and articulate church historians and theologians of our time. In spite of a dizzying array of responsibilities, Carl agreed to labor with us to remind fellow believers of our ongoing need of Christ and of our shocking privilege of an audience with the Almighty through the gospel. Carl is a professor of Church History at Westminster Theological Seminary in Philadelphia, PA. He is a lover and defender of the gospel, and I'm certain that his contributions will be good for Christ's church.

I'm thankful for Joe Tyrpak. For almost eight years we were blessed to labor together at Tri-County Bible Church in Madison, OH. Upon my move to Killian Hill Baptist Church in Lilburn, GA, Joe took on the responsibilities of lead pastor at TCBC, and he's done exceedingly well. I miss working with him—and especially praying with him!—but I rejoice that the Lord has multiplied our ministries. Joe has been my dear friend, and my beloved pastor. He writes on prayer as one who knows it and needs it. I've knelt with him, and wept with him, and rejoiced with him in prayer. I assure you that he can teach you much.

Finally, thanks to Abby Huffstutler, who once again has edited and re-edited to make us look more coherent than we really are.

As with *Gospel Meditations for Women*, and *Men*, and *Missions*—I urge you to dive into the Scriptures themselves. These devotionals will be a poor substitute indeed for the inspired Word of God. But they'll bless you if you use them as a tool to help you in your search of the true and timeless Treasure. I pray that these meditations will help you to pray more—and pray better.

May the Lord alone be glorified (Psalm 115:1). Grace!

Chris Anderson, *editor and contributing author*

DAY 1.   I've Got Nothing

"In vain….In vain….In vain."—Psalm 127:1-2

"I've got nothing." That's one of my mantras. Walking around the church I pastor, asking for God's help as I strive to lead it well, I shrug and confess aloud that "I've got nothing." On my way to the pulpit, preparing to preach, I mumble under my breath that "I've got nothing." Even preaching to people, and urging them to run to Christ and not to me, I admit that "I've got nothing." I don't say that because I'm humble, or godly. The opposite is true. I pray it because I'm painfully aware of my frailty. I say it because it's crystal clear to me that I am urgently, deeply, desperately in need of God's grace. The answer to my needs, the needs of my family, and the needs of my church is Christ. So I pray—almost constantly—for God to do what I cannot.

That's the heartbeat of prayer, isn't it? We pray because we're convinced of our insufficiency. We pray because we know that Christ's words in John 15:5 are true: "Without me, you can do nothing." We pray because we are haunted by our impotence and humbled by God's omnipotence.

Psalm 127:1-2 drives this point home. Again and again the text reminds us how "vain" our best efforts are apart from God's work. It is *vain* to labor on a temple (or home, or church, or any other endeavor) unless the Lord is building (v. 1a). It is *vain* to defend a city (or business, or mission, or family) unless the Lord is protecting (v. 1b). It is *vain* to "rise up early, stay up late, and stress ourselves out" (my loose translation) as if we're sovereign—because we're not (v. 2a). We're weak, as evidenced by the fact that we spend one-third to one-fourth of our lives sleeping (v. 2b). We can't do it (whatever "it" is). We're not enough. We've got nothing.

So do we give up? No. We pray. We ask God to bless our labors by building our homes—both through us, and in spite of us—so that our labor isn't wasted (v. 1a). We ask God to protect our children and ministries—both through us, and in spite of us—so that our watching makes a difference (v. 1b). We pray and we work, exercising what I call "diligent dependence." And then, having done our best and having asked God to show His strength where we are weak, we *sleep*. We sleep as though God were good, and powerful, and sovereign. And He is. And He works. And He does what we knew all along we could not.

Whatever God has called you to do is too big for you. You can't plant a church. You can't raise a godly family. You can't save people. You can't grow people in the faith. You can't even grow *yourself* in the faith. You might as well embrace your limitations. Say it, out loud: "I've got nothing." Then, despairing of any hope but Christ, appeal to Him for grace—what William Hendriksen defines as "God's spontaneous, unmerited favor in action" (*New Testament Commentary: Ephesians*, p. 71). See if God's grace isn't more than sufficient for you. Labor faithfully. Pray. And then rest. Because when you've got nothing—*and know it*—you're ready to see all the "something" He's got at His disposal, for His glory.

Sufficient God, who delights to manifest Your might when we've confessed our frailty, answer the prayers of Your needy people. Overcome our weakness with Your power. Overcome our folly with Your wisdom. Overcome our sin with Your grace. And we, who have nothing in ourselves, will have everything in You, and we will be jealous to give glory to no other. Amen.—CHRIS

DAY 2.
Cry for Wisdom

"If you call out for insight and raise your voice for understanding...."—PROVERBS 2:3

Wisdom, according to the Bible, has nothing to do with how well you did on your SATs, with how many books you've read, or with your abilities in logical debate. Wisdom is a different kind of skill. (Notice in Exodus 28:3; 35:25; and 36:1 that *skillfulness* is the essential meaning of the Hebrew word *wisdom*.) Biblical wisdom is the skill of pleasing God that comes as a result of a personal, submissive relationship with Him—a relationship that affects every choice in your life.

No one comes into the world with wisdom. Instead, every person is born with "no fear of God before their eyes" (Romans 3:18)—minor league fools who, given a little time, will work their way up to the majors. Foolishness comes naturally; wisdom doesn't. Foolishness comes from within, wisdom from without.

So how does anyone get wisdom? Simple. Wisdom comes to those who pray for it. Moses asked God for it (Psalm 90:12). Solomon requested it (1 Kings 3:5-10) and taught his children to cry out for it (Proverbs 2:1-6). Jesus commanded His disciples to ask, seek, and knock for it (Matthew 7:7; note the context of the chapter), and James urged believers to pray for it (James 1:5). Notice that a life of wisdom does *not* come in answer to a one-time, apathetic prayer for it; rather, wisdom comes to those who persistently and passionately beat down the door of heaven for it! And, when people today cry out for wisdom, God gives them Jesus, Jesus, and more Jesus.

Only those who come to God through Christ are wise. Wisdom begins with the fear of the Lord (Proverbs 1:7; Ecclesiastes 12:13), which refers to a relationship with God on the basis of repentant faith. Job explained it that way: "The fear of the Lord is wisdom, and turning away from evil is understanding" (Job 28:28). New Testament Christians understood the core of wisdom the same way, only with clearer definition: "repentance toward God and faith in our Lord Jesus Christ" (Acts 20:21). Wisdom begins with a personal relationship with God (Proverbs 10:9), and the only way to God is through Christ. The fear of the Lord equals faith in Jesus. Sinner, cry out: "Give me Jesus!"

Only those who know Christ are wise. Jesus Christ is the Wisdom of God incarnate. He was "filled with wisdom" and "increased in wisdom and stature" (Luke 2:40, 52). He preached that wisdom comes to those who build their lives on Him (Matthew 7:24) and that He is "something greater than Solomon" (Matthew 11:19; 12:42). Many who heard Jesus talk responded in amazement: "Where did this man get this wisdom?" (Matthew 13:54). Christians are those who trust in the crucified Messiah as the wisest, most glorious Design in all of history (1 Corinthians 1–2). And, throughout life's trials, Christians remain assured that "in [Christ] are hidden all the treasures of wisdom" (Colossians 2:3). In the end, every believer will ascribe all wisdom to the enthroned Lamb (Revelation 5:12; 7:12). So, wisdom equals knowing Jesus. Believer, may the ever-increasing cry of your life be, "Give me Jesus!"

Only those intoxicated with Christ's Spirit are wise. Paul urged Christians to walk wisely, not foolishly. He explained: a wise person studies the Spirit-inspired Word, is sensitive to the indwelling Spirit's leading, and thus will be intoxicated with God's Spirit (Ephesians 5:15-18). And, just as drunkenness with alcohol leads to foolish debauchery, drunkenness with the Spirit leads to saturation with Christ: talking about Him to others, singing to Him with others, trusting Him in trials, and humbly submitting to others like He did. That's no surprise since the Spirit's job is to magnify Jesus. So, wisdom equals Christ-saturation. Christian, cry out for the Spirit's control: "Give me Jesus!"

O Lord, I'm a sinner, a fool. Forgive me through Christ. Help me to grow in grace and in the knowledge of the One greater than Solomon. Spirit, control me and conform me to Christ's image. Give me Jesus! Give me Jesus! Give me Jesus! All for His glory. Amen.—JOE

DAY 3. Compassion for the Unclean

"Taking her by the hand he said to her, 'Talitha cumi,' which means
'Little girl, I say to you, arise.'"—MARK 5:41

Mark 5 is a chapter of great uncleanness. There is the man who is literally occupied by a legion of unclean demons and who lives among the tombs in an area where the local economy is built on pig breeding. That is about as unclean as you can find. Then there is the poor woman who is perpetually menstruating and thus rendered perpetually unclean. Finally, there is the little girl who has died. Corpses—and death—are the ultimate of the ultimate in unclean things.

We need to understand the implications of this uncleanness. An unclean person in Israel could not touch anyone else, either directly or indirectly, without spreading the contamination and rendering more people unclean. If the demoniac had ever had friends, they would long since have gone, for who could risk being around an unclean madman? If the woman was married, she could not have made love to her husband, or even have held his hand for many years. More likely, if she had ever been married, she would now be utterly alone. And the little girl had been torn from her family. The sorrow there needs no further comment.

Yet, with each of these unclean characters, Jesus had direct contact. We are specifically told He touched the little girl. That should have made Him unclean, but it actually made her clean. The woman touched Him. Old Testament law is clear that that, too, should have made Him unclean, even though the contact was not intentional on His part. He should have been made unclean, but she was made clean. And while we are not told that the demoniac touched Jesus, a natural reading of the passage would seem to imply that there was contact.

Perhaps as you read this you feel unclean. Maybe you have looked at a webpage you know you should have avoided. Maybe you spoke badly to your spouse or your children. Maybe you did something that makes you feel dirty. The Devil's oldest trick is to tell people like you that they are too dirty for God, that this time they have gone too far and cannot turn to God because they will make God dirty. That is a lie. As this chapter shows, when the dirty is touched by the divine, the divine is not sullied, but the dirty is made clean.

As you pray today, reflect on these incidents, and not simply on the amazing cleansing that took place. They are truly wonderful and point clearly to Christ as Savior. But reflect also on the compassion of God which these stories display. Christ not only saved these people; He touched them. He accepted them in their filthy condition. The woman that had perhaps neither touched nor been touched by anyone for many years was allowed to touch God manifest in the flesh, and was called by Him "daughter." That is a deep revelation of the heart of God Himself, one that invites us to come to Him despite our filth, and one that demands that we respond to Him with worship and adoration.

Lord God and Father, You know me better than I know myself. You know the darkest corners of my mind and the blackest secrets of my heart. You know that even my highest deeds of righteousness are as filthy rags before You. Lord, may Your Spirit teach me repentance, and may I reach out in faith and touch Christ through Your Word. May I thus be made clean and stand before You clothed in the glorious robes of Christ's own pure righteousness. Amen.—CARL

DAY 4. 𝔓𝔯𝔞𝔶 𝔱𝔬 𝔱𝔥𝔢 𝔉𝔞𝔱𝔥𝔢𝔯

"Your Father knows what you need before you ask him."—MATTHEW 6:8

In Matthew 5-7, the Lord Jesus introduced the "platform" of His kingdom. He didn't speak of defense, or taxation, or healthcare. He spoke against hypocrisy ("be not as the hypocrites") and in favor of private piety ("go into your closet"). He spoke against religious formalism ("you have heard") and in favor of heart righteousness ("but I say unto you"). He spoke against materialism ("you cannot serve God and mammon") and in favor of spiritual investment ("seek first the kingdom of God"). All the while, again and again and again (sixteen times in the three chapters), He pointed His hearers to God as their heavenly Father, especially in His instructions about prayer: "Pray like this: 'Our Father who art in heaven.'" Generally speaking, biblical prayer is directed to God the Father—which is amazing. Think about it:

When we say, "Our Father," we pray to a God who is great (6:9-10). The audience of true prayer is God—not our peers, despite the perverse performance of hypocrites who use prayer as a stage (6:1, 6, 18). We make too little of this astounding idea: in prayer we are addressing God, who is in heaven. He is transcendent, far above us. And yet…

When we say, "Our Father," we pray to a God who is relational (6:9-10). The God to whom we pray is *knowable*—a *Father*. Beyond that, He is *ownable*—*our* Father. Prayer is principally the enjoyment of God Himself. We seek His face, not just His hands. We delight in His presence, not His presents, as A. W. Tozer states so unforgettably in *The Pursuit of God*: "Lift up [your] heart unto God with a meek stirring of love; and mean Himself, and none of His goods." Prayer is relationship, not just requests.

When we say, "Our Father," we pray to a God who is attentive (6:8, 26, 32). Jesus repeatedly reminds us that our Father knows what we need. This, Christ says, should end anxiety. God has a track record. For thousands of years He has made the sun rise on the evil and the just. For thousands of years He has clothed the fields. For thousands of years He has fed the birds. And we matter more. Though He delights in our requests, we don't need to inform Him. He knows what we need.

When we say, "Our Father," we pray to a God who is generous (6:1, 4, 6, 18; 7:7-11). God is benevolent. He delights to reward His children (6:1, 4, 6, 18). He gives only good gifts (7:7-11). Jesus says that the example of our earthly fathers should teach us as much. Jesus' allusion to earthly fathers reminds me that as kind as my dad is, I have a far greater Father. For others, tragically, Jesus' allusion brings to mind a negligent or abusive father. In either circumstance, however good or bad our earthly father may be, we have a perfect heavenly Father.

When we say, "Our Father," we pray to a God who is forgiving (6:12-15). Jesus tells us to ask our Father to forgive us. The Father is glad to answer such requests—but only from His children. Not all people have the joy of calling their Creator their Father, and not all people have the relief of forgiven sins. Only those who have repented of their sins and trusted Jesus Christ as Savior can address God as "Father" (John 1:12). Those who don't yet know Christ are instead called children of this age (Luke 20:34), children of disobedience (Ephesians 2:2), children of wrath (Ephesians 2:3), children of darkness (1 Thessalonians 5:5), and even children of the Devil (John 8:44). If you know Christ, rejoice that He has made His Father *yours*. And if you don't yet know Christ—*what are you waiting for?*

Father, thank You for knowing us and loving us anyway. Thank You for adopting us and treating us as Your beloved children. What astounding love! We love You in return, and we pray that others will as well. Amen.—CHRIS

DAY 5. 𝕻𝖗𝖆𝖞 𝕭𝖎𝖌

"That you may be filled with all the fullness of God."—EPHESIANS 3:19

Paul's prayer in Ephesians 3:14-21 may contain the biggest prayer request in all the Bible, even bigger than Joshua's commanding the sun to stand still (Joshua 10:12-14)! Paul believed that God could do more than he even dreamed. What was Paul's *gigantic* prayer in Ephesians 3? Paul prayed that a normal, gospel-preaching church comprised of saved sinners from the city of Ephesus would be filled with all of God's perfections. That's all.

Pray big—that your church family would know Christ's fathomless love. In this Trinitarian prayer Paul prays that the Messiah would be at home in believers' hearts. The moment that you turned from sin and accepted Jesus as Savior, He took up residence in your body through the Holy Spirit. (As Paul teaches in Romans 8:9, if Christ doesn't dwell in you, you're not a Christian.) However, Jesus should be able to say of you, "With every year that passes, his/her heart becomes more and more 'home' to me. I'm more settled there than I've ever been." To enjoy Christ's settled presence is to know Christ's love—He forgives your frequent sins, He's patient with your slow growth, and He's committed to work in you until you look like Him.

Paradoxically, Christians need to *know* the love of Christ that *surpasses knowledge.* Christ's love is infinitely wide and long and high and deep. From Ephesians 1–3 we know that Christ's love is as wide as the Gentile world, longer than time itself, higher than the heavens from which Christ has rained down His rich kindnesses on you, and deeper than the grave where Christ went to find you in your sins. Christian, do you know that God loves you, that He's always loved you, and that He loved you even before you were created? Do you realized that He loved you even when you were under His wrath? Pray that you and your church would really grasp that love.

Pray big—that your church family would show Christ's love in all its fullness. Paul writes, "I want you to comprehend Christ's love *with all the saints.*" As John Stott aptly taught, "It needs the whole people of God to understand the whole love of God" (*Ephesians*, 137). Knowing His love is not simply a devotional pursuit, something for you to appreciate on your own. The goal of knowing Christ's love is that the whole church would be filled with all the fullness of God—that we'd be filled with the same thing that fills God—that the perfections of *God* would fill *us.* That's astounding!

What would the fullness of God look like in a church? As Paul teaches in Ephesians 4–6, a church filled with God's fullness would be humble and unified, holy and obedient, loving and submissive. Jesus essentially taught the same: that God's fullness would be evident when Christians are full of love and unity—the love and unity that exist eternally between God the Father and God the Son (John 17:26). Bottom line: a church that's filled with God's fullness looks like Jesus. (Notice how Paul uses "fullness" in Ephesians 4:13.) God's goal for Christians individually and corporately is nothing less than entire conformity to Christ, in whom all of God's fullness dwells bodily (Colossians 1:19; 2:9).

Unity. Holiness. Love. Complete Christlikeness. Do you think that God could ever do that in your church? He most definitely will. How much do you think He can do on this side of glory? Pray today that God would do beyond what you dream. Pray big.

Father, help me and all the saints in my church to comprehend Jesus' love—that He loved us when we were dead and that He is committed to love us to the end. May we know Your love and show Your love, so that when outsiders are present with us, they'd see Your love, Your holiness, and Your unity in us. Lord, I'm doubtful that I or my church will ever be what You desire. We're so far from what we should be. Lord, I believe; help my unbelief! Do beyond what I can imagine. For Your glory. Amen.—JOE

DAY 6. 𝕹ot for 𝕸erit—𝖂e 𝕳ave 𝕹one

"We do not present our pleas before you because of our righteousness,
but because of your great mercy."—DANIEL 9:18

In a hymn titled "A Triune Prayer," I've written the following:

Blessed Father, hear our cry.
Cast out sin, but draw us nigh.
Not for merit—we have none—
For your mercy, for your Son.

Those lines contain what I believe to be the most important lesson I have ever learned about prayer. Prayer doesn't depend on my merit. On my best day, I don't deserve an audience with God. And on my worst day, I'm not denied it. Prayer is based entirely on the finished work of Jesus Christ. I approach my Heavenly Father in spite of myself and because of my Savior. I'm accepted in the Beloved—given the very privilege of communion that belongs to Christ, of Whom God said, "This is my beloved Son, with whom I am well pleased" (Matthew 3:17; 17:5). Through the miracle of justification, God now says that of *me*, entirely because of Jesus' imputed righteousness. (I've written on this in the article "Start Your Prayers in Jesus' Name" in *Gospel Meditations for Women*.) There is an entire theology behind this idea. We have access to God through Christ—not only at conversion, but throughout our Christian lives. The New Testament teaches this often. But the verse that has pinned this concept into my brain was penned some 600 years before Jesus' birth (Daniel 9:18).

To pray well, we despair of our own worthiness. Daniel is one of the godliest men in history. No bad word is said about him in the Scriptures. Even his enemies came up with no dirt on him, despite their best efforts (1:8; ch. 6). Yet, his prayer in Daniel 9 is a model of humility. In a passionate confession of guilt and justification of God, Daniel includes himself among his guilty countrymen (9:3-16). We don't pray because we're righteous. We're not.

To pray well, we cling to the character of God. Daniel appeals to God's mercy (9:9, 17, 18). He acknowledges that all that we bring to the salvation equation is the sin. So prayer is offered in spite of our vice and because of God's mercy. Any hope of answered prayer rests in the character of God, not man. "O God, we're guilty, but we appeal for *mercy*, and we cling to it as our only hope."

To pray well, we pray for the glory of God. Beyond appealing to God's mercy, Daniel appeals to God's name. That's consistent with prayer throughout the Bible. Research, and see if it's not true. The Psalmist prays for God to act for His name's sake. For His glory. For His reputation. Elijah prays for fire to fall from heaven so that it will "be known...that you are God" (1 Kings 18:36). The prayer that is motivated by God's name calls out to God and asks to see His glory: "Work, God. Flex. Show Your might. There's more at stake here than our comfort, or provision, or even salvation. We are called by Your name. So act, for Your name's sake" (vv. 15, 17, 19). Daniel closes his fervent prayer with a barrage of desperate requests that I can hardly read without a sob: "O Lord, hear; O Lord, forgive. O Lord, pay attention and act. Delay not, for your own sake, O my God, because your city and your people are called by your name" (v. 19). Is it any wonder that God answered such a prayer?

O God, we lack the integrity of Your servant Daniel, but we do echo his prayer. We make no claim to righteousness. We appeal instead to Your mercy, made incarnate in Your Son. Hear us. Help us. Forgive us. Not only for our sake, but because we are Your people, called by Your name, connected to Your glory. Hear and answer our prayers, for Your own sake. Amen.—CHRIS

DAY 7. Call Upon the Name of the Lord

"At that time people began to call upon the name of the LORD."—GENESIS 4:26

If Genesis 3 describes the Fall, Genesis 4 describes the Splat, the sad story of God's orderly world turned really messy. It opens with Cain. His name essentially means, "This is the one!" It reveals the high hopes of his parents (4:1). No doubt their hopes were dashed by the time Cain's younger brother Abel—whose name means *emptiness*—was born. Instead of being the hoped-for Man to crush the beast (3:15), Cain turned out to be beast-like. The sin in his heart was like a wild animal, "crouching at the door," ready to pounce on and devour him (4:7). Instead of killing his sin, Cain killed his brother. Cain's actions revealed a heart that was full of pride and anger—he wanted to do things his way and resented God for not accepting him. His heart was jealous and murderous—he couldn't stand the unfavorable comparison to his younger brother, yet he preferred to dispose of his brother rather than obediently sacrifice a lamb. His heart was cold and callous—he acted as if his sin and his brother were no big deal, and, despite God's remarkable grace in protecting his life, Cain fled "from the presence of the LORD and settled…east of Eden" (4:16). What a mess!

East of Eden the mess got *worse*. There Cain had children of his own, and the contagion of sin went pandemic. Here's how bad it got: Lamech, Cain's great-great-great grandson, defined marriage his own way, took justice into his own hands, and had three sons who made it big in business—buying and selling tents, trumpets, and tools (4:17-24). Does that description of pandemic evil sound a bit tame to you? (The business ventures of Lamech's boys remind me of John's description of the business world in Babylon where the merchants sold jewelry, clothes, furniture, and food [Revelation 18:11-13]). Seriously, what's so bad about making tools? The grievous problem with Cain's descendants is that they went on with their merry lives, apathetic toward their Creator! They loved life away from the presence of the Lord. So, Cain established his legacy east of Eden: a highly civilized, godless society.

The last two verses of Genesis 4 reveal the only hope for this atheistic civilization: Adam and Eve's third son, Seth, from whom the promised Serpent-Crusher would be born. Instead of running from God's presence like Cain, Seth established a legacy of people who "called upon the name of the LORD" (v. 26). Since then, humanity has been divided into the same two groups: those who avoid the Lord and those who call on Him.

"Calling upon the name of the LORD" is the only hope for those living east of Eden. It involves knowledge, faith, and prayer. The only way you can "call upon the name of the Lord" is if you *know* what His name is. God's name is "I Am" (in Hebrew, *Yahweh* or *Jehovah*). "I Am" reveals that the God of this universe is absolutely unique, undivided, unrivaled, uncreated, undying, unchanging, and unaided. On this side of the incarnation, knowing "the name of the LORD" includes understanding that Jesus is the great I Am—the One Whom Seth, Noah, and Abraham worshiped, and before Whom Moses and Joshua took off their shoes (John 8:58; 19:4-8). However, you need more than mere knowledge. You must also have *faith* in God's appointed Sacrifice. In the Old Testament, "calling upon the name of the LORD" always took place at "an altar" (see Genesis 12:8 and 26:25), because forgiveness of sin and a relationship with God are made possible only by the blood of a Substitute. On this side of Jesus' cross, you can be reconciled with God only through faith in Jesus' once-for-all sacrifice (Acts 4:12; Romans 3:24-25). Knowledge of God's name and faith in God's Sacrifice give birth to *prayer* for God's deliverance. If you have never "called upon the name of the LORD," do so now (Acts 2:21-41; Romans 10:9-13).

Lord Jesus, You're the great I Am. I'm a guilty sinner in need of deliverance. I believe that God, Your Father, accepted Your sacrifice on my behalf. I believe He proved it by raising You from the dead. I submit to You as my Lord. I call on You now: Save me! Amen.—JOE

DAY 8. Praying through Depression

"Why are you cast down, O my soul, and why are you in turmoil within me?"—PSALM 42:5

Discouragement—even depression—is a normal experience for God's people, and prayer is the normal road on which God's people travel through it. Psalms 42-43 were written by the sons of Korah, the temple gatekeepers in Israel. Korah's children had been graciously saved from the fierce wrath of God that was poured out on their father, all his friends, and their children (Numbers 26:9-11). These men went through life—like everyone should—thinking, "I deserve to be dead." The man who wrote these psalms (notice they're written from an individual's perspective), though a privileged recipient of God's grace, was depressed. Why? Because he was being deported: he was traveling through Hermon, crying under enemy jeers, remembering Israel's "glory days," yearning for the time when he'd return to the temple (42:2-6; 43:2-4, 9-10). He wrote these psalms during the exile, the lowest point in Israel's history. He teaches us how to pray when we're despondent.

Pray through the valley of depression. The words of Psalm 42-43 were prayed in the wake of Israel's failure, in full view of God's just judgment, and with complete recognition (from Jeremiah's preaching) that Israel's immediate future would remain dismal for decades. Yet, Israel could sing these songs of hope as they marched in chains to Babylon. You, too, can prayerfully sing through the darkest times of your life. These psalms, like the whole psalter, were written for God's people of every era to sing (Ephesians 5:19). Isn't it encouraging to know that you can pray in the valley? When you feel spiritually dry, deserted, and bewildered, don't lose heart. If God's people could sing after the temple had been looted and destroyed and after Jerusalem had been torched, then nothing can happen to you that will be beyond the reach of the words, "Hope in God." Look *up.* Remind yourself: "My God lives; the LORD is my Savior, my life, my rock, my refuge, and my exceeding joy" (42:2, 5, 8, 9; 43:2, 4). Hope *in God.*

Listen to Jesus pray through the darkest valley. There's even more encouragement in recognizing that Jesus prayed through the valley better than you ever will. *As you pray Psalm 42:1-2* ("As a deer pants for the water brook, so pants my soul for God"), recall the desperate cry of Jesus from the cross—"I thirst" (John 19:28)—and remember that Jesus, your Lord, knows what it's like to experience dryness in the soul. *As you pray Psalm 42:3* ("My tears have been my food as people continually say, 'Where is your God?'"), recall that men passed by the Man of Sorrows mocking, "He trusts in God; let God deliver him if He really delights in Him!" (Matthew 27:43). Jesus, your Lord, knows taunting. *As you pray Psalm 42:4* ("These things I remember as I pour out my soul"), hear Jesus recounting the glory He enjoyed with His Father before the world existed (John 17:5). Jesus, your Lord, knows what it is to endure thoughts of "the way things used to be." *As you pray Psalm 42:5* ("Why are you cast down, O my soul, and why are you in turmoil within me?"), recall that Jesus' soul was "exceeding sorrowful even to the point of death" (Mark 14:34). Jesus, your Lord, knows what it's like to have a downcast spirit. *As you pray Psalms 42:9 and 43:2* ("Why have you forgotten me?…Why have you rejected me?"), consider the worst cry in history, as the Son of God bore our revolting sins: "My God, my God, why have you forsaken me?" (Matthew 27:46). Jesus, your Lord, knows what it's like, not just to feel like God has turned His back on Him, but for God to actually do it. You'll never experience that, since He did.

The God in Whom you're hoping is not distant from your times of dryness and desertion. He faced deeper darkness than you ever will, and He came through. So, as you pray, keep hoping in God even if your life seems depressingly dark.

Lord, I deserve to be dead, but You saved me from Your wrath. You are my salvation. I long to worship in Your very presence, for You are my exceeding joy. Lord Jesus, until I see Your face, keep my ears attuned to Your song in the valley. You are my rock. Amen.—JOE

DAY 9. Jesus, Risen and Interceding

"Since then we have a great high priest...."—HEBREWS 4:14

Christians rightly place much emphasis upon the life, death, and resurrection of the Lord Jesus Christ. These things are, after all, the objective basis of our salvation, which is then made real to us as individuals through the work of the Holy Spirit. Sometimes theologians speak of redemption accomplished and applied: the Son accomplishes redemption, the Spirit applies it. There is a lot of truth in that phrase, but there is also a sense in which it can, taken out of context, be misleading, especially if it is read as saying that the Son drops from the picture once His earthly work is done. That is not the case: the Son is as active in the application of our salvation as He was in its accomplishment.

Understanding the intercession of Christ is important to a balanced biblical theology of the Christian life and of prayer. A few weeks ago, I was talking to one of the local Eastern Orthodox priests. "The problem with you Protestants," he said, "is that you focus so much on the death of Christ, you forget about the resurrection." As a pastor, I reflected on what he said: I felt that he had indeed highlighted a weakness in my own preaching, and I wondered what I might do to ensure a more biblical emphasis in the future. The conclusion to which I came was this: Spend time reflecting upon the intercession of the ascended Christ. One of the glories of the New Testament is its teaching that Christ is alive now, interceding for His people at God's right hand. And, of course, the basis and content of that intercession is His death and resurrection. A focus on His intercession should result in a more balanced approach to His death and resurrection.

Too often we think our own prayers are weak and ineffective; and we think thus because we assume that their efficacy depends upon us. This is not so. The prayer of the greatest saint is but the faintest shadow of the Son's prayers; by itself it is useless. Yet, joined to the intercession of Christ, the faintest prayer of the weakest Christian is powerful because it is perfected and presented to the Father by His perfect, obedient, divine Son. And the Father delights to hear and to grant the requests of His Beloved.

As you pray today, draw comfort from Christ's intercession. It is powerful because Christ as God only asks of the Father what the Father Himself most deeply desires. It is powerful because it is built upon Christ's death and resurrection. It is powerful because Christ as Priest has taken human flesh and knows the weakness of the same. He can therefore sympathize with us even as He speaks to His Father. We should thus pray boldly, knowing that our prayers will be heard. Perhaps they will not always be answered in the way we expect or desire. But they will be answered wisely by the One whose foolishness is so much wiser than our wisdom. And we know that the answer will be the wisest and best because the High Priest who offers them is Christ Himself, the beloved Son of the One who hears them.

Father, forgive us for the way in which we often pray in our own strength, either seeking to make You beholden to us or doubting because we know our own weakness. Teach us through Your Spirit to look not to ourselves but to Your Son, Who sits even now at Your right hand and makes intercession for us. May we learn to rest in His work for all things. Amen.—CARL

DAY 10. 𝕻𝖗𝖆𝖞 𝖋𝖔𝖗 𝕸𝖊, 𝕻𝖗𝖆𝖞 𝖋𝖔𝖗 𝖄𝖔𝖚

"Is anyone among you suffering? Let him pray."—JAMES 5:13

Life is messy—especially life alongside other people. It's even messy in the church. In the letter that bears his name, James corrects fellow Christians for hypocrisy, including significant inter-personal issues. Favoritism in the church. The abuse of money. Discord between the "haves" and "have nots." Gossip. Complaining and competing. So how does James culminate this book that keeps warning against selfishness and disunity? With a rather abrupt call to prayer and fellowship. James commends a church culture that encourages transparency so that we can support one another in corporate prayer. He urges "share for prayer."

Share your afflictions with your church family so they can pray with you (5:13a). Christians suffer, sometimes as a result of their faithfulness (James 1:2). Although our natural tendency is to respond to hardship with complaining, discouragement, or resignation, James points us to Christ: "Is any one among you suffering? Let him pray." Let adversities chase you *to* Christ in prayer, not *from* Him in bitterness. And, in light of the verses that follow, run to Him with other believers.

Share your joys with your church family so they can pray with you (5:13b). If we respond to affliction with prayer, how shall we respond to blessings? With prayer—perhaps sung. In both circumstances, the right response when "life happens" is prayer, whether a prayer of petition or a prayer of praise. And again, based on the context of the verse, it makes sense to make this *public* praise—singing in harmony. Both blessings and sorrows are made to be shared. It has been well said that "shared joy is a double joy. Shared sorrow is half the sorrow."

Share your illnesses with your church family so they can pray with you (5:14-15). Of course, I'm not urging you to share your germs. Don't infect people—just inform them. James commands us to let each other know when we're sick, and especially to let our spiritual leaders know. (Don't wait for your pastor to call you, secretly punishing him if he doesn't; James tells you to call him!) We don't just pray; we pray *together*. Prayer is a corporate exercise. Contrary to the "stiff upper lip" mindset of many, sometimes the most spiritual thing to do is to request help. Get your church praying with you! Perhaps the Lord will be pleased to bring healing, for His glory. If not, your church family will be ready to help you suffer well.

Share your sins with your church family so they can pray with you (5:16-20). This is where people start getting nervous. However, James tells us that transparency with the right Christian friends isn't dangerous—it's safe. Vulnerability with your friends reduces vulnerability with your enemies. Sometimes the best way to fight sin is to drag it out of the dark and ask fellow believers for help. Welcome the accountability and prayer support of faithful friends. If you're in a good church, they'll pray for you, not condemn you. The prayers of trusted friends may keep you from sinning—and may help reclaim you when you do (vv. 19-20).

James calls us to deep fellowship. To vulnerability. To relationships. To prayer. Mark Miller, a dear friend and fellow elder for many years, has captured the idea this way: *"Pray for me, pray for you."* Those six words have become a motto at both churches I've pastored, shortened in our text-crazed age to PFMPFY. God intended for us to care for each other, pray for each other, rejoice with each other, weep with each other, and restore each other. Whether you're afflicted, happy, sick, or sinful, prayer is always the right answer. Especially prayer with fellow believers. PFMPFY.

Thank You, Lord, for the blessing of the local church. How kind You are to give us brothers and sisters with whom we can share our lives—helping one another, praying for one another, and praising You with one another. May my church be a loving, sharing, burden-bearing family, for Your glory and our good. Amen.—CHRIS

DAY 11. 𝕬𝖍𝖊𝖓 𝕵𝖊𝖘𝖚𝖘 𝖂𝖆𝖎𝖙𝖘 𝖙𝖔 𝕬𝖓𝖘𝖜𝖊𝖗

"When he heard that Lazarus was ill, he stayed two days longer."—JOHN 11:6

Lazarus was sick. Mary and Martha asked Jesus to intervene. And, *because* Jesus loved Lazarus, He *waited*. Jesus does the same to you: Many times He leaves you hanging, waiting for an answer. Why? Sometimes, He doesn't answer because of unconfessed sin in your life (Psalm 66:18; 1 Peter 3:7). But when sin's not in the way, why no answer? John 11 provides a perfect case study on unanswered prayer.

Jesus knows your request. Jesus knew that Lazarus was sick even before the messenger came from Mary and Martha (John 11:3). Later on, He knew that Lazarus had died without anyone telling him (11:11). When Jesus delays to answer your prayer, remember that He knows what you're asking for. He's not hard of hearing. He's not ignoring you. Christian, Jesus knows you—He knows when you stand up and sit down (Psalm 139). He knows the exact number of hairs on your head (Luke 12:7). He knows your needs before you ask Him (Matthew 6:8). Even when Jesus doesn't respond like you wish He would, it's not because He's oblivious. He knows.

Jesus loves you. Jesus stayed two days longer *because* He loved this family (11:5-6). It's the same with you. He shows His deep affection for you by giving you what's best for you. What's best for you? Stronger faith, deeper joy, broader advance of the gospel, and greater wonder at Jesus' glory. Jesus often gives you all of these by *not* immediately answering your prayer. It's all for your good. He's always doing what's best for you, even when He seems absent.

Jesus grieves with you. Jesus' delay resulted in Lazarus' death. Mary, who had urged Jesus to respond sooner, was left to grieve her loss. Jesus' apparent lack of responsiveness to your prayers has the same effect: you're left to suffer and (often) to cry. But, notice that when Jesus saw Mary weeping, He didn't stand by with an I-know-what's-coming smirk. Rather, He was "deeply moved" and "greatly troubled," and He "wept" (John 11:33-35). When Jesus sees His loved ones suffering, He's both empathetic toward them and disturbed over the hardships they suffer. Even when you're crying over prayers Jesus didn't answer, you can be certain: "His heart is touched with [your] grief" (from Frank Graeff's hymn, "Does Jesus Care?").

Jesus will be more glorified for delaying. "Lazarus, come out!" (John 11:44). Jesus spoke the command, and every onlooker saw the glory of God (John 11:4, 40)—in a more dramatic, more public, more obvious way than if Lazarus had simply gotten well. He let the situation get darker so His glory would shine more brightly. With a word, Jesus finally answered the sisters' prayers—more gloriously than they ever imagined. In a moment, He dried their tears—and dropped their jaws. Mary and Martha would not have wanted to repeat their experience, but they wouldn't have exchanged it for anything. They couldn't have improved Jesus' plan or timing, and for the rest of their lives, Mary and Martha would recount how they witnessed God's glory.

Christian, Jesus has conquered the grave—Lazarus' grave and His own. So every time He doesn't immediately answer your prayer, be certain that it will eventually end for you the same way it ended for Mary and Martha: in greater glory for Jesus Christ. If you value Jesus' glory, then you should value unanswered prayer, confident that the Son of God knows you, loves you, and grieves with you, and that He's going to be more glorified for delaying than if He had answered right away. Wait, trusting Him.

Lord, help me to trust You when You're silent. When You wait to answer my prayers, assure me of Your love and empathy, and give me strong confidence that in the end You're going to be more glorified because You delayed. "Teach me the patience of unanswered prayer." I pray in the name of the One Whom the Father always hears. Amen.—JOE

DAY 12. Pray Doxologies

"To the King of ages, immortal, invisible, the only God, be honor and glory forever and ever. Amen."—1 TIMOTHY 1:17

Paul commanded Christians to pray comprehensively: "at all times…with all prayer…with all perseverance…for all the saints" (Ephesians 6:18). In saying "with all prayer," Paul meant, "I want you to pray with *all kinds* of prayer" (NIV). Have you ever considered how many kinds of prayer there are? There's adoration, thanksgiving, supplication, intercession, imprecation, confession, benediction, and—a fairly unusual kind of prayer—doxology (literally, "a word of glory"). A doxology is prayed when a believer says, "God, I want You to be glorified." This kind of prayer appears at least fourteen times in the New Testament letters. (For a few glorious examples, see Romans 11:33-36; 16:25-27; Ephesians 3:20-21; 1 Peter 5:10-11; Jude 24-25; and Revelation 1:5-6). The men who had been eyewitnesses of God's glory *loved* to pray for God's glory.

Sadly, praying doxologies is quite rare in our churches and in our closets. Do doxologies seem strange to your ears—almost like stiff liturgies? Maybe that's because you don't pray them often. It might also be that doxologies don't make sense to you—you're praying for something that's a permanent fact. It could seem as pointless as praying for the sun to rise tomorrow. You may think, "If nothing can improve God's glory or change it, why should I pray for it?" Consider three reasons for praying doxologies.

God saved you to praise His glory forever. Paul writes of himself, "I used to scoff at the name of Christ. I hunted down his people, harming them in every way I could" (1 Timothy 1:13, NLT). Yet the grace of Jesus Christ *overflowed* for Paul (1:14), and he became a billboard advertisement for sinners (1:15-16). Everyone who saw Paul's life could say, "If Christ could save a wretch like him, I know He can save a wretch like me." Just the thought of being saved made Paul pray a doxology: "To the King of ages, immortal, invisible, the only God, be honor and glory forever and ever. Amen" (1:17). Every time you think of how God saved you, you should pray, "God, be glorified!" After all, God saved you to praise His glory (Ephesians 1:6, 12, 14). Think of your conversion, and pray a doxology—right now.

God Himself is unceasingly glorious. God is glorious in His *authority*: He is "King of the ages…the blessed and only Sovereign, the King of kings and Lord of lords" (1:17; 6:15). God is glorious in His *life*: He is "immortal," and He stands alone in that category (1:17; 6:16). God is also glorious in His *essence*: He is "invisible," and His being radiates "unapproachable light" (1:17; 6:16). No created being can see God in His essence nor approach His direct presence. Even holy angels must cover their faces. God Himself is glorious. So, since God has always been and will always be this glorious, you should *never* stop ascribing glory to Him (Psalm 104:33). In view of who God is, give Him the glory He deserves by praying a doxology.

God will be glorified throughout eternity. Although He's all-glorious, "at present, we do not yet see everything in subjection" to Him (Hebrews 2:8). Sin and death still exist. The world, the flesh, and the devil don't see His glory. But when Jesus returns to earth (6:14-15), He will judge His foes, establish His kingdom, and God's glory will fill the earth "as the waters cover the sea" (Habakkuk 2:14). Throughout eternity God's glory is going to render the sun unnecessary (Revelation 21:10-11, 23). All of history is moving toward the full display of God's glory on earth. It's going to happen. So, until God's glory fills the earth, you can show your confidence in and longing for God's glory on earth by praying for it—often. Even now.

God, You are the only King. You're blessed—enthroned in joyous praise. You're immortal; I'm not. You're unapproachably holy; I'm unholy. Yet You, my King, became a Servant—my Savior. Be forever exalted! May I never stop praising You! Amen.—JOE

DAY 13. Pray in the Power of the Spirit

"The Spirit himself intercedes for us with groanings too deep for words."—ROMANS 8:26

The world in which we live is beautiful—and broken. There are macroscopic problems: earthquakes, tsunamis, floods, and droughts. There are microscopic problems: AIDS, cancer, Alzheimer's, birth defects, and miscarriages. Perhaps most grievously, there are human problems: prejudice, estrangement from children, divorce, murder, and war. Louis Armstrong's "wonderful world" is awash in suffering, and it groans.

Romans 8 deals with life in a broken world as helpfully as any passage of Scripture. It addresses the Christian's struggle with sin and suffering, answering both evils with the finished work of Christ and the ongoing work of the Spirit. In the middle of this masterpiece chapter, Paul teaches us about the role of the Holy Spirit in prayer.

We read in verses 19-22 that creation groans beneath the curse—a curse it was dragged into against its will by human sin (v. 20). If you're not convinced that the creation groans, watch a little Animal Planet, preferably with a young child. See if you're not soon comforting her about the lion who ate the wildebeest, the snake who devoured the mouse, or the spider who sucked the life out of its guest. Creation groans. But Paul says that we—Spirit-indwelt Christians—groan, too (v. 23). We know all too well the sting of loss and the longing for our final redemption when Christ will fix this mess. Indeed, there are times when we can't even pray. All we can muster is a sigh, or cry, or moan. That's all we've got, like Job (Job 3:24), or David (Psalm 5:1; 38:8-9). In such times of too-deep-for-words sorrow, the Spirit is active in at least three ways:

The Spirit groans with us. If you're paying attention, verse 26 should surprise you. Sure, creation groans as it suffers. And yes, Christians groan, with pain and expectancy, just like a mother in labor. We get that, both by teaching and experience. But verse 26 says that the *Spirit* groans. Think about that. Why would God the Spirit groan? He's not suffering loss. He's not confused. So why? As best I can understand it—and it's a truth that is deeply comforting to me—He groans in *empathy* with the redeemed. When we suffer, He shares our suffering, like the wise companion who cries with a mourning friend rather than offering counsel. The Spirit groans because we groan. Astounding.

The Spirit translates for us. Thankfully, the almighty, all-wise Spirit does more than empathize with us. He helps us. He prays with us, with "groanings that cannot be uttered" (KJV). That's not a prayer language. It's not a heavenly dialect. Rather, it's His gracious work to translate our wordless prayers into intelligible requests. When we don't know what to pray (v. 26), He knows the perfect will of God (v. 27), and He edits our prayers accordingly. He takes our messy requests and improves on them, turning our groans of "straw" into prayers of "gold," Rumpelstiltskin-like.

The Spirit intercedes for us. Beyond editing our prayers, the Spirit prays on our behalf. We think of the Lord Jesus as our great Intercessor—and He is (v. 34)! But we have another Intercessor who prays for us on earth while Jesus prays for us in heaven.

Thank You, Spirit of God, for Your ministry to us. We would be dead in sin without Your saving work, and we would be benighted in confusion without Your sanctifying work. Whether we pray with eloquence or sighs, we know that You are enabling and improving our prayers. So we pray in pencil, relying on You to convey our prayers to the Father in the ink of His will. Amen.—CHRIS

DAY 14. How to Pray on Your Darkest Day

"O LORD, how many are my foes!"—PSALM 3:1

It was the worst day of David's life—and that's saying a lot. It was worse than any day you can imagine. We read about it in 2 Samuel 15-16. David was running for his life—not from Saul, or the Philistines, but from his own son, Absalom. He was in peril of losing his kingdom, as much of the nation he had built rallied behind the *coup*. His family was in danger. He was forsaken by trusted advisors. He was viciously mocked by accusers. He left his beloved Jerusalem in mourning. Barefoot. Weeping. With gravel and insults hurled upon him. It was a personal and national crisis that in some ways foreshadowed the eventual expulsion of David's greater Son from that same city a millennium later (John 19:16-17; Hebrews 13:12).

How should the believer respond to such a day? The Bible doesn't leave us to imagine our own answer, for Psalm 3 was the inspired prayer-song David composed while reflecting on that dark day. Read it, and learn from it how to pray in your most agonizing hours.

Acknowledge your troubles in prayer (v. 1-2). Many believe that prayer requires a Pollyanna optimism. But God doesn't call us to deny reality, or even to deny our heartache. Many of the Psalms are songs of *lament*, that pour out sorrow to God in what seems almost like a complaint. Are we allowed to do that? Apparently so, since the inspired hymnbook is filled with it. Carl Trueman explains the danger of pseudo-spiritual optimism this way: "A diet of unremittingly jolly choruses and hymns inevitably creates an unrealistic horizon of expectation which sees the normative Christian life as one long triumphalist street party—a theologically incorrect and pastorally disastrous scenario in a world of broken individuals" (*The Wages of Spin*, 159). In Psalm 3, David laments to God about his foes—which were "many" (used three times in v. 1-2).

Affirm God's goodness in prayer (v. 3-4). David was honest about his troubles. But he didn't allow his trials to chase him *from* God. Rather, they chased him *to* God. Whatever was at the root of David's hardships (and in this case, it was due in part to his own sin), he resisted the urge to doubt God's goodness. Yes, life might stink right now (v. 1-2). "*But You…*" (v. 3). He turned the corner. He appealed to God as his Shield (in the midst of danger), as his Glory (in the midst of shame), and as the Lifter of his head (in the midst of depression). And when he called, God answered, as He always does (v. 4)—contrary to the taunts of our foes (v. 2).

Find rest in prayer (v. 5-6). In the midst of chaos, surrounded by thousands of assailants, David found rest—both literally and spiritually. His problems weren't resolved, but his heart was at peace, relieved of fear. Confident in God's sovereign care, he slept, then awoke, sustained by Jehovah (v. 5). The experience of many a believer has been that running to Christ results in rest.

Rejoice in salvation in prayer (v. 7-8). Psalm 3 is a short Psalm. As a result, it makes hairpin turns in a matter of moments, though they may have taken David more time to maneuver in real life. Whether it records a succession of thoughts or the back-and-forth of doubt and faith, it ends with the expectation of triumph. David calls on God to "Arise," and to "Save" (v. 7a). God is never seated in passivity, but sometimes it feels that way. David calls God to action—even to breaking the jaw of the wicked (v. 7b). God did so in David's life. He may do so in ours, and He may not. But David's Son, the Lord Jesus, certainly broke the jaw of Satan through His death and resurrection. And the result—in eternity, if not in time—is salvation and blessing for His people (v. 8). Grace!

Lord, at times life seems unbearably hard. Thank You that You understand that, and invite us to bring our frustrations to You, unfiltered. Thank You for Your goodness, even when we don't deserve it. Thank You for shelter. Thank You for rest. Thank You for owning and sharing salvation. We trust You. We praise You. We run to You. Amen.—CHRIS

DAY 15. Get Good at Coming Clean

"Wash me thoroughly from my iniquity, and cleanse me from my sin!"—PSALM 51:2

At times godly saints fail royally. King David stayed home from war, lusted for and slept with Bathsheba, ordered her husband to be killed, then went on for several months thinking he got away with it (2 Samuel 11-12). God, out of committed love for David, sent the prophet Nathan to confront him, and, after almost a year of hardened hypocrisy and hiding from God, David broke down. He repented, and God immediately forgave him (2 Samuel 12:13). This royal failure resulted in Psalm 51, a model of good confession

Good confession is helpless (v. 1-2). The words, "Have mercy," evidence David's desperation. He was saying, "I have nothing else! If You're not merciful, Lord, I'm condemned!" All good confession begins with helplessness. Like David, you must beg God for mercy, knowing that He has steadfast love and abundant compassion on sinners.

Good confession is honest (v. 3-6). It's self-indicting. Like David, be fully aware that *you* have sinned. Admit that your sins were ultimately against God Himself, and that you were responsible for your rebellious actions. When David said, "In sin my mother conceived me," he wasn't blaming his mom. He was saying, "What I've just done is *totally consistent* with my nature." When you confess your sin to the Lord (and others, for that matter), be totally honest. Say it like it is: "My sin is all my fault."

Good confession is hopeful (v. 7-12). Healthy confession is helpless, honest, then remarkably hopeful. Like David, you anticipate full restoration: restored *purity* after filth, restored *joy* after brokenness, a restored *closeness* with the God Who has been hiding His face, restored *consistency* in your walk with God, restored *empowerment* for ministry, and restored *tenderness* in a heart that's been stubborn and hard. You don't simply want to be rid of guilt; you want to be fully restored in fellowship with God through Jesus' sacrifice.

Good confession involves holy ambition (v. 13-19). David wanted forgiveness because he wanted to be a testimony of God's grace. Like Paul a thousand years later (1 Timothy 1:16), David knew that God wanted to use him as an example for God's people, to display just how forgiving God is! So you should seek forgiveness with a passion for future ministry. Isn't it interesting that Psalm 51 is in the Bible? It's actually a specific answer to David's prayer for usefulness in verse 13. Clint McCann reflects: "The chief among transgressors and sinners is now the teacher of transgressors and sinners. The reconciled bears the message of reconciliation" (*A Theological Introduction to the Book of Psalms*, 106). Good confession is not just personally focused; it's kingdom-focused, desiring the advance of God's fame as He pours out His grace on His precious people.

I began using Psalm 51 as a pattern for repentance almost twenty years ago. I'd open my Bible, set it on the floor in front of me, get on my knees, and pray each line, applying it to my failure. Throughout years of use I've found that it cuts through my excuses and my desire to maintain self-respect (which so often accompany my attempts at confession), and it strikes at the root of my sin. Psalm 51 has helped me to repent of my sin, but it's also helped me grow through failure. If, as Martin Luther famously put it, "Jesus…called for the entire life of believers to be one of repentance," then biblical repentance is part of growing in grace. Through Psalm-51-like confession, you become more sensitive to sin, more ashamed of it, more abhorrent of it, and more amazed at God's grace in forgiving you of it.

Lord, my life is failure upon failure, yet You are the God of steadfast grace. You have forgiven me of all my sin through Christ, and since then You've shown me nothing but grace—grace upon grace. Lord, I've sinned against you again. I offer no excuses. I plead Your grace. Forgive me. Wash me. Restore me. And, I pray that You'd still use a royal failure like me as a trophy of Your grace. Through Jesus. Amen. —JOE

DAY 16.

Shut Up and Listen

"Behold, I am of small account; what shall I answer you?
I lay my hand on my mouth."—JOB 40:4

Job can be a daunting book to read. Its subject matter (the suffering of the innocent) and its form (poetry) make it fascinating, beautiful, but often difficult. Students of the book also disagree over where the turning point in the drama occurs. Is it with the hymn to wisdom in Chapter 28? Is it with the speeches of the young firebrand Elihu? Or is it when God Himself enters the scene, clothed in the whirlwind?

I would suggest that one good contender for the "turning point" award is Job 40:4, when Job decides it is time to shut up and keep silent. That is perhaps hard for us to understand today. We live in a world marked by noise. The ubiquity of information technology means that we need never really sit in silence: we can watch the television, look at the internet, chat on Facebook, talk on the phone, tweet and text to our hearts' content, all while listening to our iPods. Yet, for all the noise we make, it is arguable that very little of any substance is actually said. The noise of our lives is perhaps more often than not simply a clever way of disguising their essential emptiness. It is time to recover the importance of silence.

By Chapter 40, Job has spoken and heard a lot of speeches. Yet it's only really the last speech that makes an impact—the first speech of God Himself. Confronted with the terrifying majesty and sovereignty of God, Job realizes at last that it is time to shut up and listen. Yes, he has suffered horribly; yes, his mind no doubt reels with grief and teems with questions; but the answer is ultimately listening to the speech of God. And that answer, as readers of the book of Job know, is not a direct answer to any of Job's questions but rather an assertion of God's almighty and glorious character.

When reading the Book of Job, we should always bear in mind that, however remote Job, his problems, and his questions might seem, there will come a day when they, or something very like them, will be ours. If you live long enough, you will lose loved ones: a parent, a spouse, perhaps most terrible of all a child. Job's cries of agony and his questions about God's justice will on that day become the very words we utter. At that time, cry out as we might, the only real comfort will come not from our own utterances, but from hearing God Himself speak. And though He may not give us specific answers to our questions, He will point us towards the resurrection, the ultimate answer to all of our suffering and death (Job 19:25-26).

As you pray today, perhaps it is time to consider saying less in your prayers and spending more time listening. As Christians, we should typically start our prayers by reading the Word of God and listening to what He says there. This is no empty mysticism: prayer comes often as a response to what God has first spoken. That was one of the key lessons which Job had to learn. His world seemed very large and important until he came face to face with God; after that encounter, I have no doubt that the pain, physical and emotional, still left its scars; but his priorities were dramatically changed.

Lord God, forgive me for the many times I have been quicker to speak to You than to listen. Teach me to hear Your Word attentively and even now start to prepare my heart for listening to You in life's most painful and final moments. May Your Holy Spirit point me always to Christ, Your final Word, and may I find in Him both forgiveness of sins and hope for the resurrection. Amen.—CARL

DAY 17. 𝔓𝔯𝔞𝔶 𝔣𝔬𝔯 𝔒𝔱𝔥𝔢𝔯𝔰' 𝔓𝔢𝔯𝔰𝔢𝔳𝔢𝔯𝔞𝔫𝔠𝔢

"May you be strengthened with all power, according to his glorious might,
for all endurance and patience with joy."—COLOSSIANS 1:11

Christian, as you grow in your knowledge of Christ and His Word, you will also grow in how you pray for other believers: your prayers will sound increasingly like Bible prayers. How did Paul pray for other Christians? He continually expressed thankfulness to God for their testimony of faith and love (Romans 1:8; Philemon 4-6; 1 Corinthians 1:4-9; 1 Thessalonians 1:2-3; 2 Timothy 1:3-5). He also prayed that believers would experience brighter illumination (Ephesians 1:15-23; 3:14-19), deeper love and discernment (1 Thessalonians 3:12; Philippians 1:9-11), and increased fruitfulness (2 Thessalonians 1:11; Philemon 6). (By the way, D. A. Carson's *A Call to Spiritual Reformation* is immensely helpful for better understanding and imitating Paul's intercessory prayers.)

In the first chapter of his letter to them, Paul told the church at Colossae that he constantly prayed that they'd be filled with the knowledge of God's will (1:9). Such understanding would inevitably result in *strength to persevere* (1:11). So, in addition to those "more exciting" requests (like growth and love and fruitfulness), Paul also prayed that Christians would simply endure—that they'd keep on persevering. His example in prayer should affect how you pray for your brothers and sisters who are being tried.

Pray that Christians will be filled with the knowledge of God's will (1:9). Although God's will can refer to anything and everything God wants, here Paul is referring to something very specific, namely, God's will that all fullness dwell in Jesus (1:19). God willed Christianity to be Christ-centered. Jesus is preeminent—preeminent in His Father's heart, preeminent in our salvation, preeminent in God's revelation, preeminent in all creation, and preeminent in the church (1:13-23). And since Jesus is preeminent, preaching Him is sufficient for Christian ministry (1:24-29) and union with Him is all that any believer will ever need (2:1-15). For the Colossian believers—some of whom were toying with mysticism, legalism, and asceticism (2:16-23)—knowing God's will in this specific sense was precisely what they needed. Christian, you need to pray that you yourself and the Christians around you would appreciate the preeminence of Jesus. Comprehending Christ's fullness will result in Christian perseverance.

Pray that God will strengthen Christians for perseverance (1:11). Perseverance through life's trials is not a given; it's a gift. So don't pray merely that Christians would "hang in there." Christians don't have what it takes *within themselves*. God is the source of "glorious might." So, pray that the Almighty would give His children strength to keep going (Psalm 29:1, 11).

Pray that Christians will persevere with joy (1:11). God gives Christians strength, not just to make it through their trials, but to *rejoice* through them. Stoic endurance may be admirable, but endurance with joy is supernatural. Pray that Christians would persevere with joy—joy that's rooted in thankfulness for God's forgiving grace, in your secure citizenship in Christ's unshakable kingdom, and in hope in seeing Jesus' glorious face (Colossians 1:12-14, 27). Perseverance with joy shows that God's saints are applying to their situation the preeminence of God's Son. So, Christian, pray that you'd persevere with joy, and pray specifically for the suffering believers around you—that they'd know God's will so that they'd be strengthened to persevere with joy.

Lord, thank You for what You've done in the lives of believers in my church: You've given them faith and love. Help that testimony to persevere and to grow through trial. I pray that You'd fill my church with a knowledge of Your will. Give us eyes to see that Jesus Christ is preeminent—that He's all we need for living a life that's fully pleasing to You. Lord Jesus, may the joy of knowing You be our strength! For Your glory. Amen.—JOE

DAY 18. Spiritual Suffocation

"Pray without ceasing."—1 THESSALONIANS 5:17

Try not to breathe. Go on. Try to go 20 seconds without inhaling. It's difficult. It's uncomfortable. And if you kept at it, it would be fatal. Why? Because breathing is a natural impulse, both an *evidence* and *sustainer* of life. We do it all the time: 12 times a minute, 720 times an hour, 17,280 times a day, 6,307,200 times a year. We breathe without thinking or trying—until we're choking, we've had the wind knocked out of us (remember that feeling?), or we're dying.

That's the way prayer should be. Prayer is the breathing of the church. To "pray without ceasing" as Scripture commands in 1 Thessalonians 5:17 is to take spiritual breaths, without which we will suffocate. Sadly, spiritual suffocation is the experience of all too many Christians and churches. We have spiritual asthma. We're gasping for oxygen. We wheeze out an occasional prayer, but not freely, and not as a habit of life. Perhaps most tellingly, we think of prayer as a duty—as though we're doing God a favor each time we fill our spiritual lungs through prayer.

We need a radical shift in our understanding of prayer. To be self-congratulatory on the rare occasions when we do pray is as delusional as expecting a reward every time we exhale. No, we pray out of necessity—not because we're noble, but because we're desperate. Not because of strength, but because of weakness. Why pray? Why *breathe*? Because our lives depend on it.

Isn't that what the early church experienced throughout the book of Acts? They prayed without ceasing, devoting themselves to prayer as one of their four basic functions (2:42). They prayed while they waited (1:14). They prayed when they chose leaders (1:24; 6:6; 14:23). They prayed when they were threatened (4:23-31). They prayed when they were persecuted (7:59-60; 12:5, 12). They prayed when they sent out missionaries (13:1-3; 20:36; 21:5). They prayed—at every time, in every place, and in every circumstance.

Isn't that what Paul exemplified in his letters to churches and their leaders? He opened with prayers of thanks. He continued with prayers for spiritual progress— sometimes shifting from instruction to intercession so seamlessly that we hardly notice the transition. He prayed at the end of his letters, climaxing them with doxologies to Christ and blessings on Christ's church. Prayer was second nature to him. Like breathing.

Isn't that the point of the command to "pray without ceasing" (1 Thessalonians 5:17)? Inhale; exhale; repeat. Start the day with a spiritual yawn of thanksgiving (vv. 16 and 18). Ponder the day's agenda with a prayer of dependence. Pray as you get dressed, asking the Spirit to produce His fruit in you. Pray with your family over breakfast. Pray as you sit in traffic. Pray as the phone rings, asking for wisdom for whatever the call may be. Pray when you're tempted—then in confession when you've fallen or in gratitude when you've stood. Pray for open doors for the gospel, at work, or at your son's ballgame. Pray as you pull into the driveway, mindful of God's provision. Pray as you doze off at night. Pray without ceasing—the way you breathe.

O Lord, forgive our prayerlessness. Teach us that our lack of joy and strength stems from spiritual suffocation. Remind us how desperately we need You. Make us long for You more than the air that gives us life. Stir us to perpetual prayer, and thus restore us to spiritual vitality. Amen.—CHRIS

DAY 19. 𝕻𝖗𝖆𝖞 𝖋𝖔𝖗 𝕲𝖔𝖘𝖕𝖊𝖑 𝕬𝖉𝖛𝖆𝖓𝖈𝖊

*"Brothers, pray for us, that the word of the Lord may speed ahead
and be honored."*—2 THESSALONIANS 3:1

Prayer was the very heartbeat of the Apostle Paul's ministry. He trumpeted the need for prayer for Christians and churches over forty times in his epistles. He prayed often for others, and he occasionally asked others to pray for him. When he did request prayer, he urged Christians to pray for gospel advance. Paul wrote 2 Thessalonians to a suffering, persecuted church, and he wrote it from a tough new missionary outpost in a city called Corinth. "Brothers, pray for us" (3:1). He had been so discouraged during his time at Corinth that the Lord Himself appeared to him to encourage him (Acts 18:9-10). He described his church-planting ministry in Corinth as one characterized by weakness, fear, and much trembling (1 Corinthians 2:3). Faced with such an enormous task, Paul wrote an inspired missionary prayer letter and asked fellow Christians to pray.

We must pray with Christians, as peers. I love that Paul—the great Apostle—wasn't above asking for prayer. He called the Thessalonian Christians "brothers" and asked for their help. If he needed prayer support, how much more do we? There is no bravado in prayer. There is no feigned independence. Rather, we humble ourselves before God *and each other.* "Brothers, pray for us."

We must pray for gospel advance. Paul's request evidenced a gospel-centered ambition. He wanted the Word of God to "run." The gospel is pictured as an athlete exerting himself to make up ground. We pray for speed, for freedom, and for lack of hindrances. We're praying for *traction*—that the gospel will have great affect in people's lives, that the turf on which it runs will be ready for it. We're praying for hearts. We're praying that the Word of God will be honored. We're praying for God to work in our church, then repeat that work abroad.

We must pray for the protection of gospel ministers. Where there is advancement of the gospel, there will be opposition. Ministry isn't safe. Where there are open doors, there are many adversaries (1 Corinthians 16:9). Where there is progress, there will be pushback. Count on it. So Paul, as self-forgetful as he was, asked the church to pray for the safety of him and his missionary team (1 Thessalonians 3:2)—not merely for their sake, but for the future advance of the gospel among the unsaved. How we must pray, then, for those on the front lines! Pray for physical safety from persecutors. Pray for spiritual safety from Satan, from the world, and from our own flesh—perhaps the worst enemy of all.

When the Baptists in England were preparing to send missionaries to India in the 18th century, Andrew Fuller described the opportunity thus: "There is a gold mine in India; but it seems as deep as the center of the earth; who will venture to explore it?" The answer came from William Carey, now regarded as the father of modern missions. "I will go down," he said. "But remember that you must hold the rope." As we think of those risking their lives for gospel advance, we must hold the ropes, especially through prayer.

Christ, we pray for the advance of the gospel. We pray that it will run and be honored, and we do so because we know that we are utterly dependent on You to convict, to draw, and to save. We pray with a sense of discontentment, longing that more would come to know Your great salvation, and dissatisfied because so many are strangers to Your love and grandeur. We are astonished by Your grace. We are ambitious for Your glory. So we ask, Lord, that Your gospel will run, tirelessly, around the world. Win, Lord Jesus! For the sake of Your name. Amen.—CHRIS

DAY 20. Father, Forgive Them

"Jesus said, 'Father, forgive them, for they know not what they do.'"—LUKE 23:34

After being betrayed, abandoned, denied, condemned, and mocked, Jesus' first instinct was to pray for His enemies' forgiveness. Jesus could have justly prayed, "Father, condemn them because, in spite of all the obvious proofs of My glory, they have rejected Me." But, rather than magnifying their guilt before God, Jesus chose to minimize it, and, rather than yearning for God's vengeance and personal vindication, Jesus desired that God forgive His enemies. J. C. Ryle observed that Jesus' prayer to forgive His enemies was "probably spoken while [He] was being nailed to the cross, or as soon as the cross was reared up on end. It is worthy of remark that as soon as the blood of the Great Sacrifice began to flow, the Great High Priest began to intercede" (*Expository Thoughts on the Gospels*, vol. 2, p. 467). A few responses are appropriate for those who behold such awesome forgiveness.

Worship Jesus for the glories of His forgiving love. No one forgives like God (Micah 7:18-20). No one. It's what makes Him so glorious! David prophesied that *all the nations* would worship the Lord for the glories of His forgiving goodness (Psalm 86:5-10). When Moses heard about the glory of Jehovah's forgiveness of sins, he immediately put his face to the ground and worshipped (Exodus 34:6-8). You who used to be Christ's enemy, behold your crucified King praying for the forgiveness of those crucifying Him, and fall to the ground. What you see there is the unveiled glory of the holy God.

Rest in Jesus' forgiveness. Jesus' prayer for His enemies should assure you that you're forgiven. By His crucifixion Jesus was making the way for His enemies to be pardoned. Yet, He was not only making it possible. His prayer shows that He was desiring it. Jesus was speaking out of the abundance of His heart. Be assured: if you've turned in faith to Jesus, He's not reluctant to forgive you. He's no grudging forgiver. He was dying for you *and* praying for you. So, believing transgressor, watch the Suffering Servant. He "made intercession for" you even as He "was numbered with" you (Isaiah 53:12).

Proclaim Jesus' willingness to forgive. Jesus' words have the power to convert hardened sinners. Later in this same chapter, one of the thieves beside the Lord begged for King Jesus to remember Him (23:39-43). Matthew recorded that this same criminal had previously hurled insults at Jesus (Matthew 27:44). What do you think made this hardened robber change? There's no doubt that seeing Jesus pray like this played a part. He had never seen such love. Forgiving love has converting power, so emphasize it in your conversations with sinners.

Imitate Jesus by praying for others' forgiveness. Forgiven sinner, a forgiving heart is part of your new nature as God's child (Ephesians 4:32–5:2). "As the Lord has forgiven you, so you also must forgive" (Colossians 3:13), for if you remain unwilling to forgive another who wrongs you, it reveals that you yourself are not a genuine recipient of God's forgiveness (Matthew 6:15; 18:23-35). Those whom Christ forgave willingly, entirely, and permanently must forgive others the same way.

Are you having difficulty today showing forgiveness—difficulty moving past bitterness? Look again at your Great High Priest. Gaze long at the forgiving heart of Jesus. Repent of your sin, grieved that you're still such a poor reflection of the One whose image you're called to bear. Then, having repented, pray for the ones who have hurt you. Actually pray. Pray for them by name. Like Christ, pray that God would forgive them.

Jesus, I crucified You; my sins nailed You to the cross. When I consider how I respond to those who hurt me in so many lesser ways, I can't understand how You immediately prayed for my forgiveness. There is no one who loves to forgive like You! Jesus, I worship You. Open the eyes of more sinners to Your willingness to forgive them. Help me to forgive others like You forgave me. For the testimony I bear to Your holy name. Amen.—JOE

DAY 21. The God of Great Reversals

**"He has brought down the mighty from their thrones
and exalted those of humble estate."**—LUKE 1:52

The song of Mary in Luke's Gospel, the so-called *Magnificat*, is a beautiful and poetic anticipation of the ministry of Christ. Mary, having made the dangerous journey to visit her cousin Elizabeth, is astounded by Elizabeth's response to her arrival. While all of the social conventions of the day make Mary's visit an expected honor to Elizabeth (i.e., the younger showing respect to the older), Elizabeth's reaction is stunning. Elizabeth, filled with the Holy Spirit, asks why the mother of her Lord should come to her.

Elizabeth understands. She knows that something spectacular is taking place and that the ordinary rules do not apply. The coming of Christ—the coming of the Kingdom—turns all earthly expectations on their heads. This is the theme which Mary takes up so wonderfully in the *Magnificat*, as she sings of the Lord's looking to the lowly, casting down the proud, feeding the hungry, and turning away the well-fed empty-handed.

Mary's song is not only a wonderful description of the future ministry of her Son—the King who is crowned with thorns, the Victor who triumphs through death, the God whose church will be made strong precisely in its weakness—it is also a pattern for our own prayers. We should delight in the historic actions of God as we pray and worship, reminding ourselves of what the Bible story says: that God has remembered His promises throughout the ages, that He has shown in Christ His triumph over evil, and that He will bring history to a final, dramatic close when every tear shall be wiped away and every broken heart mended.

We should thus draw encouragement from Mary's prayer too. Many of us feel weak and inadequate as we pray and as we sing God's praises. Who, after all, is equal to the task? We live in a world where power holds sway: the rich, the beautiful, the influential are the people whom we would call the movers and shakers. They can influence the world in a way that those who are poor, plain, and humble cannot. The world's understanding of power is simple and straightforward: the strong have it, and the weak do not. So, who would want to be weak?

Yet the theology of the *Magnificat*—indeed, the theology of the whole New Testament—is antithetical to this. Here we see the good news that God delights to use our weakness for His greater glory. Weakness should not make us despondent; rather it should make us more dependent. We should see that God is the God Who loves the great inversion, Who delights to use the weak to shame the strong, Who uses instruments which are in themselves woefully inadequate for the task in order to make His own glorious sovereignty that much clearer. As you pray today, do not despair in your weakness; understand your weakness as the starting point for God's great work in your life.

Lord God, forgive us for the times we adopt the strategies of the world and seek power that allows us to manipulate and cajole those around us. We thank You that You delight not in the strong but in the weak and the humble, and thus we pray that You would humble us, that we might come to show forth in our own lives the glorious truth that in Your Son, the Lord Jesus Christ, You have lavished grace upon the poor of this world, and through Your Spirit have exalted them to the high honor of being called Your children. Amen.—CARL

DAY 22. Desperate Conditions Call for Desperate Prayers

"Moreover, as for me, far be it from me that I should sin against the LORD
by ceasing to pray for you."—1 SAMUEL 12:23

First Samuel 12 opens with Samuel's deep concern over Israel's condition. In this "farewell sermon" to Israel, Samuel reviews his integrity so that no one can blame him for the nation's ever-increasing problems (vv. 1-5). He recounts Israel's history—God's continual goodness and the people's continual rebellion (vv. 6-13). And he calls the nation to renew the old covenant (vv. 14-25).

Samuel, like Moses and Joshua before him, challenged Israel to obey the Law which was summed up in the first and great commandment: "Serve the LORD with all your heart" (1 Samuel 12:14, 20, 24). Yet Samuel, like Moses and Joshua before him, *knew full well that Israel was unable to do it*. Moses, who led the nation to enter the covenant with God at Sinai and then reaffirm it a generation later, knew that God had not "given [Israel] a heart to understand" (Deuteronomy 29:4). Moses prophesied about the day when the Lord would "circumcise your heart…so that you will love the Lord your God with all your heart." (30:6). And Moses concluded his final sermon telling Israel, "This commandment is not too hard for you" (30:11-14). The command wasn't too hard; the people's hearts were. Similarly, a generation later, Joshua reminded Israel of God's goodness, then challenged them to keep their side of the covenant (Joshua 24:14). When the people sincerely recommitted themselves to the Lord, Joshua replied, "You are not able to serve the Lord" (24:19). Again, the problem wasn't with God's demands; the problem was with people's hearts. In every case, Moses, Joshua, and Samuel set up witnesses against the people (Deuteronomy 31:19; Joshua 24:27; 1 Samuel 12:5). Not one of Israel's leaders expected Israel to keep her side of the covenant.

So, if 1 Samuel 12 teaches you anything, it should teach you that you have a hard heart. Exemplary leaders, miraculous signs, emotional sorrow, second chances, powerful sermons, sincere commitments, and severe warnings are not enough to get you to serve God with all your heart. You desperately need a new heart!

God calls you to love Him with everything in your being. Are you able to do that? Is it true that *responsibility necessitates ability*? Many people believe that God would never tell you to do something you can't do. In a sense they're right, and in a sense they're wrong. You must distinguish between two kinds of ability. It's the difference between "could we obey, theoretically?" and "will we obey, actually?" God's commands are not too hard. He's not asking us to jump over the moon. But we will not obey God's commands. Not without Help. We don't have the heart to.

From the time you were born, you were responsible to love and serve the Lord with all your heart. And, from the time you were born, your heart—like every other person's—was in a desperately sick condition (Jeremiah 17:9). Are you aware of your inability to keep God's commands? If you are becoming aware of your desperate condition for the first time, run to Christ, the Mediator of the new and better covenant, and desperately plead with Him for a new heart (Hebrews 8:6-13). And, if you've already repented and received a new heart, don't stop feeling desperate. You still carry the remnants of indwelling sin, and you still need God's help.

"Prone to wander, Lord, I feel it." Thank you, Lord, for giving me a new heart. Enlarge my heart so that I'll obey Your commands. Incline my heart to love Your commands. And, Lord, I beg You not to let me wander from Your commands. "Command what You will, and give what You command." Answer my desperate cries. Amen.—JOE

DAY 23. Open My Eyes

"Having the eyes of your hearts enlightened."—EPHESIANS 1:18

In 2 Kings 6, Elisha's life was threatened as a result of his prophetic ministry. Thugs from the King of Syria had been sent to intimidate and arrest him. They surrounded his home town of Dothan and brought a justified fright to his servant. But Elisha himself was anything but fearful, and his servant couldn't understand his confidence. Elisha told him that their army was bigger than their foes', but he couldn't see it. It must have seemed like a math-defying fantasy. Then it happened. Elisha prayed for God to open his servant's eyes, and when God answered, the servant saw a host of angelic warriors, with horses and chariots of fire. Before the removal of the servant's spiritual blindfold, he saw only enemies and danger; once God opened his eyes, he saw reality. God answered Elisha's prayer: "O LORD, please open his eyes, that he may see" (v. 17).

That's what happens in Ephesians 1:15-23 and 3:14-19. In two exquisite prayers, Paul asks that our eyes will be opened—our blindfolds removed—so that we will see something far better than an angelic army. He prays that we will see and comprehend the blessings that are ours through the gospel of Jesus Christ, knowing that once we do, our lives will never be the same. These inspired prayers should be models for us as we pray for ourselves, our families, and our churches. "O LORD, open our eyes, that we may see."

Paul opens his prayer in 1:15 with thanks to God for His work in His church. He then begins offering requests on our behalf in verse 17. He prays that the triune God—Father, Son, and especially the Spirit—will impart to us spiritual wisdom and revelation in the knowledge of Him (v. 17). He acknowledges that we can't know the things of God apart from the illuminating work of God. In fact, he uses that very imagery—praying that God will "turn the lights on" in our spiritual understanding, enabling us to comprehend three things: (1) the hope to which He has called believers, (2) the riches the gospel provides as an inheritance for believers, and (3) the resurrection power that brought Christ back to life and now works in and for believers (vv. 18-20). He tells us that this immeasurable power has exalted Christ, and that we, the church, are united to Him as a body to its head (vv. 21-23). He prays that we will comprehend both the immensity of God's power and the privilege we have to be joined to Him through the gospel. "Open our eyes!"

Paul offers a similar prayer in 3:14-19. This time he prays that we will be strengthened in our inner beings, again as a direct result of the triune God helping us to comprehend the riches of the gospel (v. 14-17). The result of such growth, strength, and communion will be an increased comprehension of the incomprehensibly vast love of God (vv. 18-19). It's an ironic prayer—"that you may have strength to comprehend…the love of Christ that surpasses knowledge." We'll never wrap our heads around it. We'll never fit all the ocean of God's love into the tiny buckets of our minds. But we can know more than we do, and to that end he prays. In both prayers, he asks that we might, thus enlightened, experience the fullness of God (1:23 and 3:19). He prays that we would grow in our experience of God Himself. I can't imagine a greater request. Not "God, open our eyes to facts," but "God, open our eyes to Yourself."

Christian, what we need—more deeply than provision, or health, or wisdom—is a deeper knowledge of God. May He be pleased to answer these inspired prayers!

Father, in Your mercy, show us Your glory. Show us the immensity of divine love, the immeasurable power of Christ, and the illuminating work of the Holy Spirit. We're blind without You. But we long to know You better. "O Lord, open our eyes, that we may see." Amen.—CHRIS

DAY 24.
God's Answers Exceed Our Requests

"Who is able to do far more abundantly than all that we ask or think."—EPHESIANS 3:20

Ephesians 3:20-21 concludes Paul's prayer for the church with a flourish. Indeed, it concludes the entire doctrinal portion of this exquisite epistle with one of the grandest doxologies in Scripture. Paul has been unpacking the treasures that are ours in the gospel (notice the ubiquitous "spiritual riches" motif throughout the book: 1:3, 7, 8, 11, 14, 18; 2:4, 7; 3:6, 8, 16). He has prayed that we'd come to know the infinite vastness of Christ's love (3:14-19; see yesterday's devotional). And now, as though he can't contain himself, he moves from exposition and intercession to uncorked exultation. In doing so, he teaches us still more inspired lessons about prayer.

God answers prayer better than we offer it (v. 20). I love this. There are so many ways in which my prayers are feeble. I forget requests. I omit details. And even if I know the situation well, I don't know what's the best solution. I make a request as thoughtfully and diligently as I can, but I rest in this—*God is more eager to answer than I am to ask.* And more *wise.* And more *able.* He doesn't match my requests and imagination. He exceeds them—infinitely. He's not looking for a loophole. He's not stingy, willing to show His might only if I say the magic word. He's good. He's eager. He's all-wise, all-powerful, and all-gracious, and He exercises His infinite attributes *in spite of* my prayer as much as *because of* my prayer. As Bryan Chapell writes in his excellent book *Praying Backwards*, "Faith in God's sovereignty actually causes us to rejoice that we do not bind God with the limited wisdom and mixed motives of our prayers" (p. 57). How grateful I am that God does "far more abundantly than all that we ask or think." He edits my requests. He improves upon them. He is gracious to hear, and even more gracious when answering.

God answers prayer for His glory (v. 21). Paul first describes God as the prodigal prayer-Answerer. Then he explains why God answers prayer—and why He heaps the treasures of blessings on us through Christ. What does he elect? Why does He adopt? And forgive? And redeem? And regenerate? And unite us to himself? Ephesians 1:6, 12, and 14 and Ephesians 2:7 have answered that question repeatedly and resoundingly: *for the praise of His glorious grace.* We are blessed with God's riches, by God's grace, at God's will, through God's Son—and all for God's glory. And that's the climax to which Paul ascends at the end of the doctrinal half of the book. Doctrine culminates in doxology. Teaching yields to singing. Preaching erupts into praise. Paul rejoices that God has saved us for one overarching purpose—that the church of Jesus Christ will bring God glory. Now, for future generations, and on and on into eternity. And Paul underlines this soul-stirring doxology with a hearty "Amen." May it be so. And it will be. It will happen. It is certain. God will be glorified by His blood-bought church.

So pray. Pray, knowing that God will improve on your request when He answers it. And pray with an eye to God's glory, knowing that God will answer prayer and redeem sinners and do all that He does for the glory of His great name.

Merciful, rescuing God, Your generosity exceeds our imaginations. Our words fail us. We are overwhelmed by Your lavish kindness, especially in giving Your beloved Son to save Your accursed enemies. For our Savior and salvation, we give You glory, and we always will. Amen.—CHRIS

DAY 25. Meditation : Prayer :: Hand : Glove

"How precious to me are your thoughts, O God! How vast is the sum of them!"—PSALM 139:17

God comforts you in all your affliction. Exactly *how* does He do it? Here's how He *doesn't* do it: He doesn't usually give it in a verse you've never discovered, a book you've never read, or an experience you've never had. You live in a highly individualistic culture that craves highly individualistic spiritual experiences. But God doesn't typically comfort you with something strange and unfamiliar. He usually comforts His people as they prayerfully meditate on the basic truths He has revealed about Himself.

King David penned Psalm 139, as verses 19-22 indicate, while his life was being hunted. Where did David—a grown, godly, mature man who not only knew a lot of Scripture, but wrote a lot of it!—turn to find God's comfort? Interestingly, he went to the first lessons of his "elementary Sunday School curriculum." David sought for God's comfort in personalizing simple truths about God. You should expect to experience God's comfort the same way: in prayerful meditation on the basic attributes of God.

Personalize God's omniscience (vv. 1-6). David's prayer was more than, "God, You know everything, so You must know me." Instead, he thought, "God knows me *because He has searched me.*" (The term *searched* is used of mining for gems in 2 Samuel 10:3 and Job 28:3.) God has, as it were, taken the time to descend the mineshaft of your life, explore every cave, and uncover every rock. He's examined your actions, your schedule, your thoughts, your words. Considering human sinfulness, only those who know God's forgiving grace can *take comfort* in such intimate knowledge (Hebrews 10:22); and, only Christians can affirm that God *knows* them personally (Matthew 7:23). David meditated on God's omniscience until he cried, "Such knowledge is too wonderful for me!" Has God's omniscience ever made you cry out like that? It should. Believer, don't seek for comfort "off the beaten path." Meditate on simple truth: "Lord, You know me."

Personalize God's omnipresence (vv. 7-12). When David prayed, "Where can I go from your Spirit or where can I flee from your presence?" he wasn't trying to escape. Instead, he was prayerfully thinking, "Even if I tried, I couldn't hide from You." East or west, earth or sky, alive or dead, light or dark—God's children can't escape God's guiding and protecting presence. Even when Jonah tried to run away, he couldn't escape God's storm or God's fish! Believer, nothing—not distance, death, or darkness—can separate You from God's committed love and continual presence. (I call Psalm 139 "the Romans 8 of the Old Testament.") Meditate on God's presence in prayer.

Personalize God's sovereignty (vv. 13-16). David found comfort in knowing that God was present with him in his mother's womb. These are some of the most tender and comforting verses in all of Scripture. When David was still unformed—as his bones, muscles, heart, lungs, and brain were still developing—God was perfectly ordering the construction. Verse 16, more powerfully than any verse I know, proclaims the truth that God's sovereign ordering of every believer's life is "womb to tomb." He formed you according to His plan, and He planned every day (and every trial!) of your life before you ever saw one. Christian, God's attention is on you! It was on you before you ever existed, and it's been on you every second of every day since. Chew on that in prayer.

Don't look for comfort in "exotic places." Look for it in theology that four-year-olds can grasp. Assume that you need to experience more deeply what you already know. J. I. Packer says it so well: "We must turn each truth that we learn about God into a matter of meditation before God, leading to prayer and praise to God" (*Knowing God*, 23). God comforts you with simple, prayerful meditation on Himself.

Lord, who am I that You notice me? Yet, You've studied me—all my actions, words, and thoughts—and You've chosen to love and redeem me. Your thoughts toward me are more numerous than the sand! Root out the distrust and anxiety in my heart. Amen.—JOE

DAY 26. Draw Near through Christ

"Since we have a great priest over the house of God, let us draw near."—HEBREWS 10:21-22

What comes to mind when you think of the word *cherub*? A lawn ornament? A greeting card? A painting of a bored, bared, be-winged baby? Webster defines a cherub as "a beautiful usually winged child in painting and sculpture." Well, that's cute. But it's not accurate. Cherubim aren't cherubic. They're mentioned 92 times in Scripture, and they are decidedly not cute. In fact, they are terrifying (Ezekiel ch. 1 and 10; 41:18). They are warriors, not cupids. And they are charged with keeping sinners out of God's sanctuary. Their message is unmistakable: "You cannot pass!"

Cherubim barred sinners from the sanctuary of Eden. We think of Eden as a garden—and it was. But it was much more. It was the original "holy of holies," the place where God communed face to face with Adam & Eve (Genesis 2:15-17). The best part of Eden wasn't the food, or the weather, or the landscaping. It was being with God in unhindered fellowship. Tragically, our parents preferred independence over worship. They broke God's one command, dooming all of creation with them in their devastating Fall (Genesis 3). The curse fell: sweat, pain, conflict, and death entered the world. Humanity was *estranged* from God by their own nature (3:8-10) and *exiled* from God by divine sentence (3:22-24). God forced us out of the sanctuary of Eden, and He set cherubim with flaming swords to make sure we stayed out. "You cannot pass."

Cherubim barred sinners from the sanctuary of the tabernacle and temple. Thousands of years pass before we see the cherubim again. The location isn't Eden, but the tabernacle—another sanctuary. This time the cherubim are symbolized by artistic renderings: carved into golden images and sewn into curtains (Exodus 25:18-22; 26:31-33; 36:35 for the tabernacle; 2 Chronicles 3:14 for the temple, the building that replaced the tabernacle approximately five centuries later). The cherub's role was unchanged, however. They stood guard on the veil between the holy place and the holy of holies, barring sinners from access to God. "You cannot pass!" they commanded, silently. Only one man (the high priest) on one day (the Day of Atonement) could penetrate the veil into God's immediate presence, and that only for a moment (Leviticus 16). "Eden" was still closed to sinners. Access was denied.

Cherubim were removed and access to the sanctuary was restored by Christ. Our study of the cherubim isn't trivial. This matters a great deal. It's beautiful, and it's life-changing. The Lord Jesus was the serpent-crushing, curse-reversing Deliverer promised in Genesis 3:15, just prior to the placing of the original cherubim outside of Eden. He fulfilled all of God's commands on sinners' behalf. He bore the curse in sinners' place—the very curses promised in Genesis 3: sweat, pain, thorns(!), and even death (Galatians 3:13). And in the most amazing reversal of all, He, God's beloved Son, was *estranged* from His Father—was *exiled*—so that rebels might be brought near (Matthew 27:46). When Jesus died, in the most symbolic event in history, the cherub-adorned veil in the temple was torn from top to bottom (Matthew 27:50-51). The cherubim sheathed their swords and stepped aside. Sinners were welcomed back into God's presence. Access to God has been restored by Jesus Christ (Ephesians 2:11-18; 3:12). Sinners are invited—are *commanded*—to "draw near" to God, relying entirely on Christ and His finished work (Hebrews 10:19-22). With joy and urgency, I plead with you to do it. Draw near. Make frequent use of "the new and living way" Christ has opened for us to God. Draw near now, and for the rest of your life—and never stop marveling at what Christ did to bring you to God. Grace!

Father, we deserve nothing but Your wrath. Your cherubim should execute us now and torment us forever. But in breathtaking grace, You've welcomed us back into Eden, bearing our exile Yourself through Your forsaken Son and our forgiving Savior. Amazed, we approach You through Jesus. Thank You for bringing us home. Amen.—CHRIS

DAY 27. Why Share Your Despair with Others?

"You also must help us by prayer, so that many will give thanks on our behalf for the blessing granted us through the prayers of many."—2 CORINTHIANS 1:11

Living for Christ is full of immense burdens, some of which are so heavy and constant that you, like Paul, could "despair of life" (1:8). No one is totally certain of all that Paul meant by "the afflictions we experienced in Asia" (1:8). He certainly had in mind the constant plotting of Jews to take his life, as well as the united animosity of the silversmiths in Ephesus—which is where Paul was working when he wrote 2 Corinthians. The opposition in Ephesus had broken out in a riot that nearly killed a few of Paul's teammates. (You can read all about these problems in Acts 19–20.) Paul's afflictions also included the weight of the situation 400 miles away in Corinth. One of his most strategic church plants was apparently redefining the gospel and rejecting Paul's leadership. All of these trials combined to make Paul's years of church planting efforts in Ephesus some of the worst (yet, by God's grace, some of the best) in his life. In his season of despair, Paul learned four helpful realities about hardships.

Sometimes your hardships feel unbearably heavy. It's immensely encouraging to know that someone as godly and spiritual as Paul could feel "so utterly burdened beyond [his] strength that [he] despaired of life itself" (1:8). Can you believe that? Less than a year earlier this same man had written to this same church that God "will not let you be tempted beyond your ability" (1 Corinthians 10:13). Now, Paul teaches that, although trials are never too heavy for us, they sometimes *feel* as though they are heavier than we can handle. Burdened believer, take heart. Paul, who had written 1 Corinthians 10:13, sometimes felt like 2 Corinthians 1:8. Remain firmly convinced that God is in fact limiting your trials, even though you often feel like they're going to crush you.

Your hardships should bring you to the end of yourself. Paul's afflictions made him feel certain that he was going to die; he lost all hope of life. But this wretched feeling of despair produced wonderful results: It led him to stop relying on himself (1:9). Apparently, even the Apostle Paul had seasons of ease when his daily focus quietly shifted from God to himself. Trials have a way of revealing sinful self-reliance. What grace!

Your hardships force you to rely on God. In his season of despair Paul learned to hope in "God who raises the dead" (1:9). Paul knew that God had raised Jesus from the dead, and God would one day raise all Christians from the dead. Notice how Paul was exemplary in applying the theology he knew. As Paul Barnett puts it, "It is…very easy to regard this God [who raises the dead] as remote and distant from the present situation, to think of him as the God of theology and not of reality" (*The Message of 2 Corinthians*, 34). You must know what God has done in the past, know what He's promised to do in the future, and then take the time to apply it to your despair today. Past resurrection + future resurrection = present hope. You must be able to say courageously with Paul in the face of disheartening circumstances, "God has delivered us, and He will deliver us again" (1:10; 1 Samuel 17:37).

Your hardships make you depend on the prayers of others. Paul's despair led him to depend on the prayers of others (1:11). You too must depend on the prayers of other Christians because God has chosen to multiply His glory and His people's joy in this way. The goal of prayer is not simply "problem solved," but the greater glory of God and the greater joy of His people. Take time right now to pray for the needs of another believer, and then ask another believer to pray for one of your burdens.

Lord, forgive me for my pride that often keeps me from sharing my problems with others. I don't like to admit my weaknesses to others, and I rely way too much on my own strength. Help me rely on You and on the prayers of Your people—not only so that I'll be helped, but so that You'll be glorified and Your people encouraged. In Jesus' name. Amen.—JOE

DAY 28. 𝔓𝔯𝔞𝔶 𝔚𝔦𝔱𝔥𝔬𝔲𝔱 𝔄𝔰𝔨𝔦𝔫𝔤

"Bless the Lord, O my soul, and forget not all his benefits."—PSALM 103:2

One of the most fruitful habits of my pastoral ministry has been encouraging people to pray without asking—for *anything*. It surprises people to realize that they can pray without a grocery list of requests. "What do you pray about if you're not asking for stuff?" Well, you talk about God. To God. For God. You offer prayers of adoration. Both churches I've pastored have made a "Prayer of Adoration" part of our liturgy (or "service order" for non-Presbyterians). We even occasionally make it a corporate exercise, having several people offer short prayers of adoration extemporaneously, reflecting on truths from the Scripture reading, or the morning's hymns, or their own gospel meditations. The result is always thrilling. The church is encouraged and our Lord is exalted. You need to learn to pray without asking for a single thing. Just praise.

Psalm 103 shows us this kind of prayer. It's one of my favorites. Some Psalms are arranged with a lesson in mind. Some are an extended metaphor, like Psalm 23. Some are laments, recording the writer's inspired struggles with a fallen world. But this Psalm almost feels unstructured, like the writer is expressing spontaneous praise to God in a "brainstorming" session. He repeatedly urges people (including his own soul) to "bless the Lord." And he heaps reason upon reason. "God is like *this*. And *this*! And *this*! And He does *these* things. And I love *this* about Him!" It's a great model of what prayers of praise should be. Read it, and other Psalms, looking for descriptions of God. Here's how. (I've included parts of speech for my fellow "word nerds.")

Praise God for His titles. (These are nouns.) God is called many things in the Psalms. Psalm 103 calls Him "LORD" or Jehovah—ten times! Other Psalms call him a fortress, a shield, a shepherd, a head-lifter, a defense, a savior. Recall these things. Record them. Pray them to God in praise.

Praise God for His attributes. (These are adjectives.) God is good. And great. And merciful. And forgiving. And holy. And just. And compassionate. Honor Him by rehearsing these attributes, especially as you read about them in the Psalms. And study His attributes further, using a book like A. W. Tozer's *Knowledge of the Holy*.

Praise God for His works. (These are verbs.) Notice how active God is in Psalm 103! Among his "benefits" (v. 2) are many gracious deeds: He forgives. He heals. He redeems. He crowns. He satisfies. He renews. He reveals Himself through Scripture. He removes our sins from us, as far as the east is from the west—as beautiful a description of Christ's power to cancel sin as any in the Bible. And on it goes. God acts, and He does so with gospel grace.

Here's the sum of the matter. Don't just pour out empty words. *Think*. About God. Then pray, offering Him the praise He deserves. And on occasion, intentionally omit anything but adoration. Forget yourself. Rivet your attention on God. Adore Him. Try it, and see if your heart doesn't delight in doing the very thing for which you were created.

God, there is no one like You. You deserve praise for who You are. You are unrivaled in Your majesty and mercy, Your glory and grace, Your transcendence and condescension. You deserve praise for what You do. For making and sustaining all things. For tolerating us. For making an infinite sacrifice to save us. For forgiving us. For welcoming us as Your own children. May we so delight in You that voicing prayers of adoration will be our greatest pleasure. Amen.—CHRIS

DAY 29. Pray to Christ the Conqueror

"If Edom says, 'We are shattered but we will rebuild the ruins,'
the LORD of hosts says, 'They may build, but I will tear down,
and they will be called "the wicked country,"
and "the people with whom the LORD is angry forever."'"—MALACHI 1:4

The book of Malachi is made up of six disputations, or arguments, between God and His people. The first question that the people ask is how God's claim to love them can be said to be true. It is perhaps an understandable complaint: the people had returned from exile a mere shadow of their former selves, a tiny vassal state subject to enemy rule.

Given the debased understanding of love in modern society, as preached from a myriad of soap operas, sitcoms, and commercials, we might have expected God to respond in some sappy, sentimental way: "Well, every time I think of you, I have this warm fuzzy feeling in my heart, and I get kind of nostalgic for all the good times we had together." That, of course, is not how God responds.

What He actually says is, "I destroyed your enemy Edom, and if he ever rears his ugly head again, I will chop it off without hesitation." This is not love as we are taught to understand it today, as an emotion or sentiment. This is love as action, and it is vital that we understand it as such.

The Westminster Shorter Catechism Q. 26 describes Christ's role as king in these terms: "Christ executes the office of a king, in subduing us to Himself, in ruling and defending us, and in restraining and conquering all His and our enemies." Christ's kingly role thus involves Him destroying all His and our enemies. That is not love as we typically define it, but it is a vital part of God's love for His people.

Christ's love is demonstrated supremely upon the cross. There He dealt with our sin and took the punishment we deserved. But He did more than that: He confronted our final enemy, death itself, and crushed it. When He rose on the third day, He demonstrated that death could not hold Him and also that death could not hold any who belong to Him, either. Death may be the final enemy, but it does not have the final word. God's love has the final word, destroying the destroyer, the greatest enemy of our souls.

As you pray today, reflect upon that aspect of divine love. Give thanks that God has and does destroy all your enemies. This is not to be an excuse for looking for human vengeance for petty personal grudges. It is far more important than that: it involves the destruction of your greatest enemy, death itself, in the life, death, and resurrection of Christ. Give thanks that death will not hold you. And also pray that God will allow you to love others—your spouse, your children, your friends, your neighbors—in a way that goes beyond simply intense affection and manifests itself in your passionate action to protect them from whatever enemies seek to destroy their bodies and souls. It has been said many times before but remains true: love in the Bible is really a verb, not a noun.

Lord God, You are indeed a loving, heavenly Father. Forgive us for the small thoughts we have of Your love, for our tendency to reduce it to sentiment or to merely human dimensions. Give us a truly biblical vision of Your love as demonstrated in the crushing of death, our greatest enemy, by Jesus Christ in the power of the Spirit. And as we praise You for this love, we ask that we too might show forth the same to those around us—our spouses, our children, our neighbors, and our friends. Amen.—CARL

DAY 30. 𝔄 Gospel Meditation for Pathetic Pray-ers

"Now may the God of peace who brought again from the dead our Lord Jesus,
the great shepherd of the sheep, by the blood of the eternal covenant,
equip you with everything good that you may do his will."—HEBREWS 13:20-21

Aren't you thankful that the Bible wasn't written for perfect Christians? The letter to the Hebrews was written to struggling Christians who should've been more mature than they were (Hebrews 5:11-14). And, to this day, the world has yet to see a perfect Christian (Philippians 3:12-16).

Hebrews 13:20-21 is the final prayer of this monumental letter to struggling Christians. It's a benediction, a prayer for God's blessing on His people. (The prayer ends with a doxology, too.) The core of the prayer request is this: "May God equip you with everything good." The term *equip*, as Brooke Westcott defines it, refers to "the supply of that which is lacking and the amendment of that which is faulty" (*Commentary on the Epistle to the Hebrews*, 449). Real Christians have so much in their lives that's lacking, so much that's faulty. Is your prayer life lacking or faulty? If so, you're no different from any Christian who has ever lived. You aren't perfect, and you need God to equip you. This benediction reveals how God equips you "by the blood." Here's how.

Jesus' blood fully paid your debt—so your Perfector didn't stay dead. How could God raise the One who was punished for your sins—didn't your sins deserve an *eternal* punishment? It was because Jesus' blood provided a *full* satisfaction of God's wrath. His blood had the power to satisfy the eternal wrath of God against your load of sin. His resurrection testified to the power of His blood! If the death of Jesus Christ had not fully satisfied God, God could not have justly raised Him. But God "brought again from the dead…the great Shepherd of the sheep *by the blood*."

So you have a living Shepherd whose work is described in Psalm 23: He revives, guides, comforts, and blesses you so that you can say, "I lack nothing." You have a Shepherd whose covenant-keeping love will pursue you through all your days and bring you to the Lord's house, where you'll dwell forever, faultless. Do you see how the blood relates to imperfect *you*? It ensures that your sins are entirely paid for and that you now have a risen Shepherd on whose shoulders falls the responsibility for your perfection.

Jesus' blood sealed the covenant that ensures your perfection. The covenant in verse 20 is the New Covenant. In it, God promised to perfect believers, beginning with their hearts (Hebrews 8:10-12). Notice that it's called "the *eternal* covenant." Jesus' death ratified a covenant that, as Homer Kent explains, "will never be invalidated or superseded" (*The Epistle to the Hebrews*, 293). It's eternal. And, it promises your perfection—you will be like Christ. You'll actually be able to say with Jesus, "I desire to do your will, O my God; your law is within my heart" (Psalm 40:8). The blood sealed your perfection by ratifying an eternal covenant which promised it.

Struggling, lacking, faulty Christian, don't try to improve your prayer life today. Just rest in the power of Jesus' blood. It's powerful enough to forgive you of all your sin, including your weak habits in prayer. It's powerful enough "supply what's lacking" and "amend what's faulty" in the life of a pathetic pray-er like you.

Lord, thank You for providing the Lamb to die for all my sins—including my weak prayerfulness and arrogant prayerlessness. Thank You that the Lamb arose, that my Shepherd lives, and that my Shepherd's steadfast love will pursue me all the days of my life. Thank You that You will complete the work You've begun. Lord, supply what's lacking in my prayer life. All to Jesus' glory. Amen.—JOE

DAY 31. The Bible is a Book of Prayers

"And what more shall I say? For time would fail me to tell of Gideon, Barak, Samson, Jephthah, of David and Samuel and the prophets."—HEBREWS 11:32

I hate endings. I finish reading a book, hearing an anthem, or watching a good performance, and I immediately want to go back and do it again. Yet, here we are, on the last page of a 31-day devotional. This little book packs a lot of the Bible's teaching on prayer into a small package. And yet, I hate ending it, because we've only scratched the surface. The Bible is so chock-full of prayer that it's comically impossible to exhaust the topic in a lifetime, much less in a short devotional book. I feel the pain of the writer of Hebrews when he wraps up his passage on *faith*—which, I suppose, is a passage on *prayer*—by saying "time would fail me." Indeed. So I close this little book by urging the reader to continue this study on your own. Read the Bible as a book of prayers and prayer warriors. If you're paying attention, they're everywhere. Here's an admittedly random selection of Bible stories that are saturated with prayer.

Moses was a man of prayer. Exodus 17:8-13 gives a vivid record of the power of prayer. Threatened by the Amalekites, Moses ascends the hill to pray (holding aloft the staff) while Joshua descended into the field to fight (holding aloft the sword). Both were necessary, but the staff—not the sword—determined the victor. To pray is to triumph.

Jehoshaphat was a man of prayer. In 2 Chronicles 20, he intercedes for Judah in the face of the overwhelming threat of the Moabites, Ammonites, and Meunites. God's people respond to the crisis with fasting and corporate prayer (vv. 3-4). King Jehoshaphat offers a prayer that magnifies God's sovereignty (vv. 5-12). He notes that God's name is at stake (v. 9), then concludes by acknowledging their need ("We are powerless…. We do not know what to do.") and their utter dependence on God ("our eyes are on you." v. 12). God answers with a resounding victory, using Israel's prayer and praise as though they were swords and shields.

Daniel was a man of prayer. Faced with capital punishment for praying, Daniel refuses to yield even an inch. Instead, he prays as always—windows open, three times a day (Daniel 6:10). And God delivers him from the mouths of lions, gaining great glory for Himself in the process (6:16, 20, 26).

Jesus was the Man of prayer. We have no greater example of prayerfulness than the Lord Jesus. He prayed before making decisions (Luke 6:12) and before performing miracles (Luke 11:41-42). He prayed early, before a busy day of ministry (Mark 1:35); He prayed late, after a busy day of ministry (Matthew 14:23). He taught His disciples to pray—by example, and command, and parable, and pattern (Matthew 6:5-13; 9:38; 26:41). He prayed for them the night before His crucifixion (John 17; Luke 22:31-32). He prayed for Himself, in Gethsemane, during the last hours of His freedom and before His infinite anguish (Matthew 26:36-42). And as His life was fading, He prayed still more—in mercy ("Father forgive them," Luke 23:34), in agony ("My God, my God, why have you forsaken me," Matthew 27:46), and in faith ("Father, into your hands I commend my spirit," Luke 23:46). Our Lord Jesus often healed, often taught, often suffered—but *always* prayed. And He prays for us still, even at this very moment (Hebrews 7:25).

You've completed this book. "Time fails me." But you've only begun to meditate on the life of prayer that the gospel makes possible. Dig deeper. Pray more, and pray better. Run to Christ. Enjoy Him. Worship Him. Ask Him. And rest in Him. Grace!

Blessed Father, Son, and Spirit, awaken us to the privilege of prayer. May we delight to commune with You. May we rejoice to labor with You. May we find relief in confessing to You. And may the glorious truths of the gospel embolden and inspire us to pray in faith, that You alone might be glorified. Amen.—CHRIS